DATE DUE		

I would like to dedicate this book to all of the gorillas in the world, both wild and captive, and to the people who love and care for them. I'd also like to dedicate it to the memories of the charismatic Willie B., the noble Bongo, the majestic Jambo, and the magnificent Snowflake. And happy 50th birthday to Colo, the gorilla who started it all! —NRP

Text copyright © 2007 by Nancy Roe Pimm
Cover photo by Nati Hamik/AP photo
Designed by Kelly Rabideau & John Margeson

Cataloging-in-Publication

Pimm, Nancy Roe.
The heart of the beast: eight great gorilla stories /
by Nancy Roe Pimm.
      p. ; cm.
ISBN 978-1-58196-054-9
Includes bibliographical references (p. 110–111)
and index.
Summary: Read biographies of eight real gorillas as
you learn about how gorillas are both like and
unlike humans.
1. Gorilla—Juvenile literature. [1. Gorilla.] I. Title.
QL737.P96 ?b P56 20067
599.884 dc22
OCLC: 70207463

Published by Darby Creek Publishing
7858 Industrial Parkway
Plain City, OH 43064
www.darbycreekpublishing.com

Printed in the United States of America

1 2 3 4 5 6 7 8 9

Contents

Binti Jua and Koola at the Brookfield Zoo in Chicago

1

BINTI JUA: A MOTHER'S HEART

One hot August afternoon in Chicago in 1996, a young mother sat holding her baby. Suddenly she heard a loud thud and turned to look when another mother started screaming. Nearby a small boy had just fallen from a height of almost twenty feet—and tumbled into the bottom of a ravine. The first mother, still holding her seventeen-month-old baby, headed toward the motionless child.

When she reached the unconscious boy, she picked him up and held him against her, gently rocking him. Shielding him from the inquisitive glances of curious onlookers, she turned and slowly carried the child to a secluded spot. She sat at a doorway, cradling him in her arms for a while, and then she gently placed him by the door.

Everyone who watched was surprised that this mother was protecting a youngster who was not her own. No one had expected her to bond with her *own* baby, because she had been raised without a maternal role model. For health reasons, she was taken from her mother soon after her birth. In fact, before giving birth, she was required to attend maternal training. There she learned how to feed and care for a baby with the help of a plush animal doll. An *animal* doll? This was no ordinary first-time mother—this young female was an eight-year-old western lowland gorilla named Binti Jua, which means "daughter of sunshine" in Swahili.

Binti proved to be a good gorilla mom when her baby Koola was born, but most people were shocked when they witnessed the care and compassion she showed to the three-year-old human child who had fallen into her enclosure. After safely delivering the child, Binti climbed up the rocks with Koola on her back to join the rest of the gorilla troop.

Binti Jua immediately became the focus of an international media frenzy. Reporters swarmed the Brookfield Zoo in Chicago, and news stations all over

GORILLAS AT A GLANCE

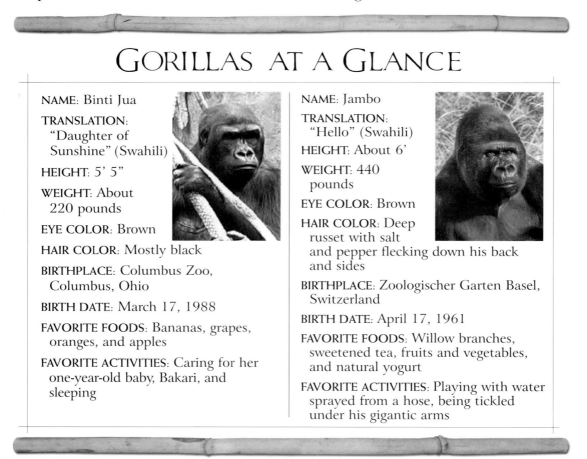

NAME: Binti Jua

TRANSLATION: "Daughter of Sunshine" (Swahili)

HEIGHT: 5' 5"

WEIGHT: About 220 pounds

EYE COLOR: Brown

HAIR COLOR: Mostly black

BIRTHPLACE: Columbus Zoo, Columbus, Ohio

BIRTH DATE: March 17, 1988

FAVORITE FOODS: Bananas, grapes, oranges, and apples

FAVORITE ACTIVITIES: Caring for her one-year-old baby, Bakari, and sleeping

NAME: Jambo

TRANSLATION: "Hello" (Swahili)

HEIGHT: About 6'

WEIGHT: 440 pounds

EYE COLOR: Brown

HAIR COLOR: Deep russet with salt and pepper flecking down his back and sides

BIRTHPLACE: Zoologischer Garten Basel, Switzerland

BIRTH DATE: April 17, 1961

FAVORITE FOODS: Willow branches, sweetened tea, fruits and vegetables, and natural yogurt

FAVORITE ACTIVITIES: Playing with water sprayed from a hose, being tickled under his gigantic arms

the world played and replayed the amazing video of the event. Letters and gifts poured in, addressed to the suddenly famous gorilla. An overnight celebrity, Binti received a medal of honor from the American Legion and an honorary membership in a California P.T.A. Later that year, *Time* magazine named her the recipient of the "Humanitarian of the Year" award—an honor no one expected a gorilla would receive!

MATERNAL INSTINCTS . . . OR MORE?

Photo by John Belhomme

Some believed that Binti Jua acted from pure maternal instincts, but a male gorilla named Jambo showed the same compassion for a human life—ten years earlier and an ocean away. One Sunday afternoon in 1986, five-year-old Levan Merritt and his father went to the Jersey Zoo, located on Jersey Island in the English Channel. A crowd watched in

Curious gorillas kept their distance as Jambo placed himself between them and the little boy who had fallen into the enclosure.

horror as Levan fell into an enclosure inhabited by a gorilla troop. The onlookers gasped as the four-hundred-pound silverback approached the unconscious boy.

Jambo—followed by his favorite female, Nandi—went down the grassy slope to where the boy lay. The other gorillas in his troop followed. Twenty-five-year-old Jambo (Swahili for "hello") was the dominant male of the group. When the younger, adventurous blackback, Rafiki, got too close, Jambo deliberately placed himself between the inquisitive gorilla and the little boy—a gesture the entire gorilla troop seemed to interpret as: "Don't touch. Stay away."

As Jambo moved closer to the boy, the crowd began to shout, "Get away, you brute!" From beneath a heavy brow, Jambo stared down at the boy who had fallen into his enclosure. Then, with his huge padded hand, he gently touched the boy's back. After touching the boy, the gorilla brought his massive hand up to his nose and sniffed it. Then he repo-

Jambo at the Jersey Zoo, Jersey Island, United Kingdom

sitioned himself and towered over the small boy in a protective manner. Levan began to stir and gain consciousness. The crowd's fear quickly turned to panic. People screamed, "Don't move! Stay still!"

The boy looked over his shoulder to stare into the eyes of the giant silverback that was peering down at him. Then young Levan began to wail. Jambo looked at the crying boy—then at the shouting crowd. The commotion seemed to frighten him, so he retreated to the gorilla house up on the hill, his troop close behind.

Judging by their gasps and screams, the onlookers must have expected Jambo to behave like a ferocious, aggressive creature. Instead, Jambo stood over the injured child, doing the job of any good silverback: protecting the young in his area.

The reactions of Jambo and Binti Jua—one male and one female—show us the true heart of the beast.

The Rest of the Story

HAIRY PEOPLE?!

Here's an amazing gorilla fact: Adult gorillas have the same number of hairs per square inch as humans—even though they don't have hair on their fingers, palms, soles, noses, lips, ears, or chests. In fact, the word "gorilla" is derived from the ancient account of a Carthaginian explorer who sailed along the west coast of Africa nearly 2,500 years ago. After he encountered these large, hairy creatures, the African natives told him *their* name for the great ape, which became the basis for

Gorillas do not have hair on their fingers, noses, lips, and ears.

the Greek word *gorillai*, meaning "hairy person." But all of this hair has a purpose—it keeps gorillas warm and protects them from biting insects.

What other characteristics do humans and gorillas have in common?

Gorillas and humans have the same number of teeth.

- Like us, gorillas have thirty-two teeth, and they have two sets during their lifetime—a baby set and an adult set.

- Under a microscope, the blood types of people and gorillas are virtually the same.

- Humans and gorillas have unique fingerprints, but field researchers also use "noseprints" to distinguish one gorilla from another. The researcher sketches the nose of the gorilla, with its identifying wrinkles or curves, and then writes notes about the animal alongside its "noseprint."

- Gorillas can contract many of the same illnesses humans do—such as arthritis, chicken pox, tuberculosis, flu, and the common cold.

Researchers can identify gorillas by their "noseprints."

- Gorillas also have five fingers, including an opposable thumb, on each hand—each with its own unique set of fingerprints. But gorillas have something we *don't* have—on each foot is a "thumb," which allows the apes to grasp items with their toes.

A gorilla hand has five fingers, including an opposable thumb.

The gorilla foot has a "thumb" that helps gorillas grasp items with their toes.

GORILLA TAXONOMY:
All in the Family

KINGDOM	*Animalia*			
PHYLUM	*Chordata*			
SUBPHYLUM	*Vertebrata* (animals with backbones)			
CLASS	*Mammalia* (warm-blooded vertebrates that give birth to live young)			
ORDER	*Primates* (includes humans, gorillas, chimpanzees, orangutans, monkeys, lemurs, and gibbons)			
FAMILY	*Hominidae* (humans and the "great apes": gorillas, chimpanzees, and orangutans)			
GENUS	*Gorilla*			
SPECIES	*Gorilla gorilla* (western gorilla)		*Gorilla beringei* (eastern gorilla)	
SUBSPECIES	*Gorilla gorilla gorilla* (western lowland gorilla)	*Gorilla gorilla diehli* (Cross River gorilla)	*Gorilla beringei beringei* (mountain gorilla)	*Gorilla beringei graueri* (eastern lowland gorilla)

RANGE MAP FOR WESTERN GORILLA SPECIES

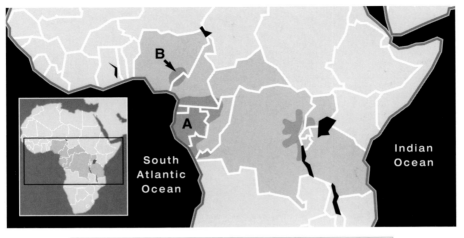

A: Western Lowland Gorilla (Gorilla gorilla gorilla)

The **western lowland gorilla** (*Gorilla gorilla gorilla*) lives in the tropical rain forests of Cameroon, Central Africa Republic, Gabon, the Democratic Republic of Congo, Angola, and Equatorial Guinea. These gorillas are the most numerous and are the only subspecies you see in U.S. zoos. Tens of thousands live in the wild, and about 550 are housed in zoos around the world. About 370 are in U.S. zoos.

B: Cross River Gorilla (Gorilla gorilla diehli)

The **Cross River gorilla** (*Gorilla gorilla diehli*) lives in five small pockets of habitat in an area on the border of Nigeria and Cameroon. The short skull, short molar row, the shape of the palate, and the shape of the skull base distinguished *Gorilla gorilla diehli* as a new subspecies separate from *Gorilla gorilla gorilla*. The current population is between 120 and 150 individuals, and none are in captivity. Conservation International and the primate specialist division of the World Conservation Union have classified this subspecies as one of the 25 most endangered primates.

RANGE MAP FOR EASTERN GORILLA SPECIES

South Atlantic Ocean

Indian Ocean

C

D

C: Mountain Gorilla (*Gorilla beringei beringei*)

The hair of the **mountain gorilla** (*Gorilla beringei beringei*) is longer and darker than its lowland relatives due to the colder climate of the high elevation. Mountain gorillas are taller and have more pointed heads and wider gaps in the middle of the nose, and they lack a reddish patch of hair on their heads, which is common in lowland gorillas.

Two separate populations of mountain gorillas, known as the Virunga and Bwindi mountain gorillas, live in the mountainous regions of Rwanda, the Democratic Republic of Congo, and Uganda. Between the two populations, approximately 700 mountain gorillas live in the wild.

D: Eastern Lowland Gorilla (*Gorilla beringei graueri*)

The **eastern lowland gorilla** (*Gorilla beringei graueri*) lives in the easternmost parts of the Democratic Republic of Congo. Because of the civil war in this area, estimating this gorilla population is difficult. Researchers believe that about 4,000 exist in the wild, and a few are in captivity. None are in U.S. zoos, however.

Colo, the first gorilla born in captivity

2

COLO: A SURVIVOR AT HEART

On the frosty Saturday before Christmas in 1956, zookeeper Warren Thomas fed a pair of western lowland gorillas, Macombo and Millie, a breakfast of mixed vegetables with an added treat of hard-boiled eggs. Millie, eight-and-a-half-months pregnant, was about to become the first gorilla ever to have a baby in captivity. Estimating that gorillas and humans have similar gestation periods, the zookeepers guessed that Millie would give birth within the next couple of weeks.

While rubbing his hands together in an attempt to keep warm, Warren observed Millie. The very pregnant gorilla usually had a huge appetite, but she was showing no interest in her food. Glassy-eyed, she moved about her cage clumsily, acting frightened and distant. Warren had agreed to meet fellow keeper Terry Strauser for coffee, but he decided to stay and take a closer look at Millie. As he walked around to the front of her cage, he was shocked by what he saw: There, lying on the cold, concrete floor was a baby gorilla!

The baby was still in the amniotic sac, its umbilical cord trailing away from it. *The first gorilla baby ever born in captivity, and it was born dead*, he thought. Warren stared at the tiny creature in its sac lying still on the ground, and he sadly reflected on how close the Columbus Zoo had come to making history.

Then the sac moved. Warren shouted in amazement, "That baby is alive!"

He raced into action, first putting Millie in a different cage, and then scooping up the dying baby and rushing her to the kitchen in the gorilla house. He broke open the sac, pulled out the tiny gorilla, and began to sponge off the female baby who was breathing sporadically. Trying to stimulate her to breathe on her own, he gave her a vigorous massage.

"I could feel her life ebbing in my hands," he says. "She wasn't doing very well breathing on her own. I had to get her lungs inflated with oxygen, and the only way I knew was with mouth-to-mouth resuscitation."

Meanwhile, Terry Strauser began to wonder why his friend hadn't shown up for coffee. He went to the ape house, only to find that he was locked out. He peered through the window and stared in disbelief at the sight of his friend giving mouth-to-mouth resuscitation to a baby gorilla!

Out of the corner of his eye, Warren could see his friend at the window, but he knew he couldn't take the time to let him in. He continued to blow air into the newborn's mouth with such zeal that he almost blew the three-and-a-half-pound baby up "like a balloon." Soon the little gorilla began to hyperventilate.

Warren stopped for a few moments to see if she could breathe on her own, but the baby continued gasping for breath. Sadly, it appeared that the newborn gorilla wasn't going to make it. Then, after one long, agonizing minute, she began to breathe normally. Warren patted the baby down with the towels and sponges he had been using and raced to the door to let his buddy in. He told Terry that the gorilla was alive but that he needed his friend's help. Warren instructed Terry to find a pair of hemostats (clamp-like instruments) to pinch off the umbilical cord. Once the umbilical cord was secured and the baby was breathing on her own, Terry and Warren finally got a chance to stare at the little miracle in the zoo kitchen.

Word about the new arrival spread throughout the zoo. Mildred Davis, the wife of Columbus Zoo superintendent Earl Davis, was one of the newborn's first admirers. She remembers being disappointed in the baby's appearance: all skin and bone, wrinkled and brown, with oversized fingers and toes attached to spindly arms and legs covered with black hair. But the gorilla's defining features were her big, dark, expressive eyes.

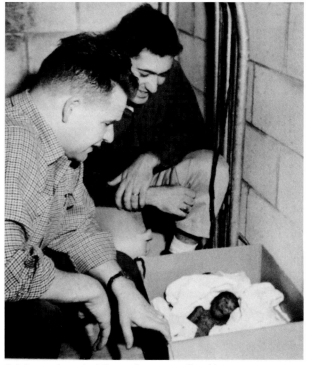

Colo lying in her makeshift nest of rags in a cardboard box.

As the news traveled around the world, telegrams began to pour in. Within a matter of hours after her birth, the *Today Show* called for an appearance. The *New York Times* printed daily updates on the little gorilla's progress, and *Time* and *Life* magazines ran stories that made the gorilla famous.

Amid all the excitement, the zoo staff focused on caring for the newborn. Afraid for the baby's safety, they decided not to return her to her unreceptive mother. The tiny baby spent her first few days, including Christmas morning, next to the heater in the gorilla house boiler room, where zookeepers had made her a makeshift nest of rags in a cardboard box. Finally, the zookeepers and the veterinarian agreed on what must be done: They would raise the infant gorilla themselves. But how? Louis DiSabato, the zoo's curator of mammals, says, "We were all animal experts, but we were writing the textbook on rearing a baby gorilla. I can remember many times we looked at each other and said, 'What do we do now?'"

A pediatrician, Dr. John Larcomb, was called to the zoo to give the three-pound, five-ounce gorilla a complete check-up. A decision was made to keep the newborn gorilla in an incubator until she grew stronger and a nursery could be built. As time went by, she showed her strength by striking her teething ring hard against the glass of the incubator. She also liked to loosen the light bulb that hung over her tiny head—a head that was no bigger than a pack of playing cards.

Once the baby gorilla was strong enough to leave the incubator, she received twenty-four-hour care by Mr. and Mrs. DiSabato, Earl Davis and his wife, and other zoo employees. They raised her the only way they knew how—as if she were a human baby.

A special nursery was built for the gorilla, complete with a crib, a changing table, and lots of baby toys. Photos of her father, Macombo, and her mother, Millie Christina, were hung on the walls. Almost every day, the baby splashed in a bath full of bubbles. Then her skin was rubbed with baby oil to keep it moist. Her diapers were changed when needed, and she had a rack full of human baby clothes.

The keepers swaddled her in a soft blanket while feeding her human infant formula, first from a medicine dropper, then eventually from a bottle. In the wild, when a baby begins to eat solid foods, a gorilla mother chews the fruits and vegetables for the baby. Then she lets the softened food fall onto her chest for the baby to eat. But this gorilla's caretakers fed her human baby food

with a spoon. And, just like a human baby, sometimes the gorilla seemed to get more food on her face than in her mouth! The little gorilla appeared to be a healthy newborn—she had a huge appetite in spite of her tiny size. But she had a nearly constant case of the hiccups, and Earl Davis suspected the baby gorilla was eating too quickly. He told the caretakers that the baby should be fed more slowly.

An overnight celebrity, Colo became the princess of the Columbus Zoo. Every Sunday she was dressed in frilly outfits and brought out to the public. People lined up to get their pictures taken with the fancy baby gorilla. For her first Easter, Colo wore her finest dress—and even a brand-new bonnet.

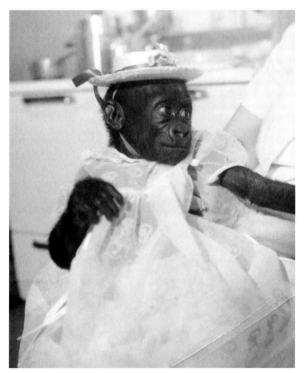

As Colo grew older, she began throwing tantrums like a spoiled child. She sometimes ran around her cage and screamed when her attendants had to leave her. In November 1957, Earl Davis wrote a letter to the city service director. In the letter, he wrote: "For Colo's future well-being, she needs animal companionship. While Colo is getting the best of care at the zoo, the nurses tend to spoil and pamper her constantly, probably to her detriment. Colo considers herself a human in thoughts and actions. She even regards her own

Colo's handlers sometimes dressed her in fancy baby outfits.

parents as odd charac-
ters." Davis went on to
say that adding a young
male gorilla would also
make a breeding program
possible. Colo only knew
humans, and Davis knew
it was important to create
a balance between her life
as a gorilla and her life
surrounded by humans.

In 1958, when Colo
was almost two-years-old,
the zoo purchased an

Her handlers often called her "Cuddles" and "Sweetie Face," but it soon became clear that the baby gorilla needed a real name. When the *Columbus Citizen* ran a "Name the Gorilla Contest," offering a prize of $150.00 to the winner, the name "Colo" was chosen—a combination of the words Columbus and Ohio.

eighteen-month-old male gorilla, captured in the jungles of what was then called Victoria, Cameroon, in Africa. Named Bongo, he arrived at the zoo on October 1, 1958.

Once Bongo had a clean bill of health, it was time to meet his new play-mate, Colo. A frightened Bongo clung to his handler, while Colo—wearing a white dress decorated with red pinwheels and triangles—jumped around and climbed the bars of her cage. Bongo appeared to be more scared than excited, and he tentatively reached out to Colo.

By March 11, 1959, the two were reportedly sleeping peacefully together, and the zoo proclaimed them to be perfectly matched. Although Colo remained attached to her keepers, Bongo became her sole playmate, giving Colo the balance she needed between the human and the animal worlds.

MOTHERHOOD FOR COLO

Ten years later, Colo and Bongo became parents. The keepers wondered if Colo would be able to care for her baby, since she had not been able to learn from her own mother. They also wondered how Bongo, a huge silverback, would react to a little one. At that time, little was known about the parenting skills of gorillas.

On February 1, 1968, Colo gave birth to a female, Emmy. One year later, she had a male, Oscar; and in December 1971, she unexpectedly gave birth to a second female, Toni. For their safety and survival, Emmy, Oscar, and Toni were removed from their parents' care and were raised by zookeepers. Just as their mother had, they wore clothes, drank from bottles, and ate baby food. The only difference was that they had each other for company.

Over the years, the zoo community compared notes as they learned more about gorillas in captivity and in the wild. One of the many lessons passed along was the importance of the troop in the gorilla world, where the old learn from the young and the young learn from the old.

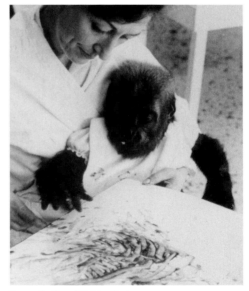

In 1987, Colo's troop consisted of a silverback named Mumbah; two females, Bathsheba and Lulu; and twin males, Macombo and Mosuba, whose father was Oscar, Colo's only male offspring. The keepers observed that Colo spent most of her time caring for the four-year-old twins. In the same year, Toni, who was Colo's

Emmy, the first of Colo's offspring

youngest, gave birth to a male, J. J. He was born on then-Columbus Zoo Executive Director "Jungle" Jack Hanna's 40th birthday. Toni lost interest in the newborn, perhaps because she, too, had been raised by humans, so the keepers took J. J. from his mother and reared the newborn in the nursery for the first year. The little gorilla needed a surrogate mom to care for him, and because Colo had been taking such good care of the twins, the keepers decided to give her a chance to be a mother to a baby.

GORILLA AT A GLANCE

NAME: Colo

HEIGHT: 5'

WEIGHT: 222 pounds

EYE COLOR: Brown

HAIR COLOR: Black

BIRTHPLACE: Columbus Zoo, Columbus, Ohio

BIRTH DATE: December 22, 1956

FAVORITE FOODS: Tomatoes and onions

FAVORITE ACTIVITIES: Spitting, drinking from a cup

Colo's maternal instincts took over when she was introduced to fourteen-month-old J. J. "Grandma" Colo immediately put J. J. on her back and behaved like any good gorilla mom. She shared her meals of fruits and vegetables and made a nest for him at night, sheltering and protecting the young gorilla as if he were her own.

The twins seemed agitated that the baby was suddenly getting most of Colo's attention. They had many screaming fits before they adjusted to the new arrival. When the twins became too rough with J. J., Colo disciplined them by coughing harshly in their faces. Macombo and Mosuba quickly learned that there were limits to their rough-housing, especially when it involved little J. J.

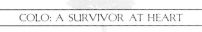

At the age of thirty-one, Colo became the first gorilla at the Columbus Zoo to become a surrogate mother. The keepers knew that Colo was smart, but they were surprised that she had such strong maternal instincts, despite not having a mother of her own to model gorilla maternal behavior.

ONE SMART GORILLA

Charlene Jendry, a conservationist and a gorilla zookeeper for more than twenty years, knows Colo well. "Colo is a very intelligent creature," she says. "Once, she found a set of plastic toy keys in her habitat. Afraid it would be a choking hazard, I tried to barter with her by offering to exchange the keys for some peanuts. Colo just gave me a look of bored disinterest. Obviously it was going to take more than peanuts to get her to surrender the keys!"

Charlene raced to the kitchen and came back with fresh pineapple. Colo looked at Charlene, then at the pineapple. After giving it some more thought, Colo finally lifted her foot, revealing the hidden keys. She picked them up, opened the ring, and took the keys off the ring one by one. The clever gorilla surrendered just one key at a time, being rewarded with a piece of pineapple for each key.

Another day, some workers accidentally left a

Colo's keepers say that she is a very intelligent animal.

metal chain in the gorilla yard. This time Charlene used yogurt as a negotiating tool. Colo pushed the chain through the fence, offering only a few links of the chain at a time. Charlene knew if she attempted to grab the chain, Colo would yank it back and easily win the tug-of-war. The keeper needed to be patient and offer an additional bite of food for each section of chain. Colo did not surrender the whole chain until the entire cup of yogurt was finished!

What Colo Taught Us

Through the years, Colo and other captive gorillas have shown us that gorillas are intelligent, gentle, and compassionate animals that should be treated with dignity. In her long life at the Columbus Zoo, Colo has taught the entire zoological community about captive gorilla breeding and development and about the emotional and physical needs of gorillas.

Colo gives J. J. a ride.

The first captive-born gorilla, Colo began her life on a cold, concrete floor where she struggled for breath. But this little gorilla had a *big* will to live. Now, fifty years later, with a noble, wizened face, she watches over her growing family. Her legacy lives on through four generations of offspring.

An ambassador of her breed, Colo has taught us the most valuable lesson of all—a gorilla needs to be a gorilla.

GORILLA FACTS:
The Rest of the Story

GREAT APES IN GREAT DANGER

Most of the early contact between gorillas and humans ended the same way—with the gorillas being killed. Due to gorillas' large, hairy appearance, people assumed they were savage monsters. Trophy hunters killed entire gorilla troops just to capture one or two babies to sell to zoos. These aggressive hunting practices drove gorillas to near-extinction.

For the past one hundred years, researchers and zookeepers have developed much more knowledge and a greater understanding of these great apes. We now know that gorillas are generally peaceful and non-aggressive creatures. They are unlikely to initiate an attack, but they will defend themselves and their troops.

Although lowland gorillas still number in the thousands, the species is seriously threatened, and their numbers continue to drop. In 1973, the U.S. Congress passed the Endangered Species Act, making it illegal to acquire gorillas from the wild. However, poachers still kill gorillas for trophies and bush meat—meat from wild animals that live in the forested land of Africa, known as "the bush." A gorilla head, for example, sells for about one thousand U.S. dollars, and a hand sells for about six hundred dollars. The hand of a gorilla is sometimes made into an ashtray.

Sadly, all viable African ape populations may become extinct due to the bush meat trade. As world-renowned primatologist Dr. Jane Goodall said in 1998, "Unless we work together to change the attitudes at all levels—from world leaders to the consumers of illegal bush meat—there will be no viable populations of great apes in the wild in fifty years."

TOOL TIME

Usually placed third—behind humans and chimpanzees—gorillas are quite intelligent. Until recently, experts thought that only humans and chimps could use tools. But ethnologists, scientists who study human behavior across cultures, observed wild gorillas in Africa using sticks and rocks as tools.

A female gorilla crosses an elephant pool using a walking stick to check the water's depth.

For example, in the Democratic Republic of Congo, a group of field researchers observed a young gorilla smashing palm nuts between rocks to extract oil. This complex behavior is known as the "hammer and anvil" technique. They also documented a female lowland gorilla using long sticks to gauge water depth while walking through a swamp pond. Another female selected a large, dead tree trunk and laid it down to cross a deep swamp patch. (The water depth is important to gorillas, because studies have concluded that they don't swim. Years ago, there were incidents in which zoo gorillas fell into moats surrounding their enclosures. They made no effort to swim, and, as a result, drowned.)

The gorillas' use of tools didn't totally surprise primate zookeepers, who had been giving their captive gorillas "food puzzles" for years. To give the gorillas a challenge and to relieve the animals' boredom, keepers sometimes stuffed a plastic pipe with peanut butter and raisins. They then sealed both ends of the pipe and placed it in the gorilla enclosure. Using sticks found in their habitats, the gorillas worked diligently to get to their food supply—and succeeded.

"We had seen our gorillas do this, as had keepers in other zoos, but because gorillas aren't known to be tool users in the wild, it was thought this knowledge of captive gorillas was not applicable," said Elizabeth Lonsdorf of the Lincoln Park Zoo. But the field reports from the Congo prove that gorillas in the wild have the same ability to use tools to accomplish certain tasks.

GORILLAS JUST WANNA HAVE FUN

Gorillas need to be stimulated by their surroundings. Many zoos include the following nonfood items for the gorillas' enrichment:

- plastic tubs, plastic stools, plastic trash can lids
- nursery toys that make noise when buttons are pushed
- wood wool (shredded trees that look like bales of straw)
- treat stands and sandwich feeders
- hammocks made of fire hoses
- cardboard boxes, shavings, or tubes
- snow
- ropes and vines
- burlap bags
- bubbles
- pieces of wood with holes drilled in
- pine cones
- balls and spools hung from the top of the cage
- milk crates
- swings
- sidewalk chalk
- shredded paper

Keepers give their gorillas balls and other nonfood objects to keep them stimulated.

A zoo gorilla plays with a milk crate.

WILD ABOUT VEGGIES!
WESTERN LOWLAND GORILLA DIET

IN THE WILD

- leaves
- nettles
- thistles
- bamboo
- fruit
- wild celery
- bracket fungus
- dock leaves
- bramble bush
- termites
- ants
- caterpillars

In the wild, western lowland gorillas consume parts of at least ninety-seven different plant species. About sixty-seven percent of their diet is fruit; seventeen percent is leaves, seeds, and stems; and about sixteen percent is termites, ants, and caterpillars.

Wild gorillas rarely drink water. They obtain moisture from the morning dew on the plants they eat, as well as from juicy fruits and some succulent plants.

Succulents are fleshy plants that store moisture in their cells and are almost half water. If an adult male gorilla eats fifty pounds of foliage per day . . . that's a lot of water!

Plants are part of all species of wild gorillas' diets.

IN CAPTIVITY

- vegetables (lettuce, green beans, kale, broccoli, onions, celery, turnips, squash, potatoes, peppers, squash, bok choy, carrots, beets, onion grass)

- monkey biscuits (similar to a Milk-Bone dog biscuit, formulated to address the special needs of a particular animal, such as being high-protein or low-fat) and monkey brownies

- strawberry muffins

- carrot biscuits

- oatmeal or pumpkin paste

- popcorn

- sugar-free toasted oats, shredded wheat, puffed rice, puffed wheat

- peanut butter (put in plastic tubes to provide a challenge for animals in captivity)

- apples, bananas, grapefruit, tomatoes, oranges

- edible flowers

- brown rice

- hard-boiled eggs

- sugar cane

- branches (The gorilla chews off the bark, which helps to clean the teeth.)

- ice blocks or ice balloons (balloons removed) as frozen treats

- Jell-O balls

- gorilla cake for a treat

Celery is one of the many vegetables that zoo gorillas eat.

Although most monkey biscuits have enough nutrition to make for a complete diet, gorillas are fed a variety of foods to increase good nutrition and avoid monotony. Based on each gorilla's nutritional needs, zookeepers also give each animal daily vitamin and mineral supplements. Twice a week in some zoos, gorillas drink special protein shakes (a blended mixture of applesauce, fruit molasses, and minerals) to promote good hair growth.

BABY BRAINS

In 1958, the husband-and-wife team of Benjamin Pasamanick, the director of research at the Columbus Psychiatric Hospital, and Hilda Knobloch, the head of pediatric psychology at Columbus Children's Hospital, were the first to study Colo. They wanted to test the first gorilla born in captivity to compare a gorilla's development to a human's. They also wanted to test the theory that the longer a species spends in infancy, the more intelligent it will become as an adult. Their theory was based on the fact that a human, the world's most intelligent animal, spends the longest time in infancy.

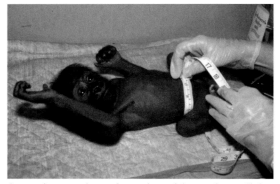
One way keepers and researchers understand the growth rate of baby gorillas is to measure them at regular intervals.

The study began when Colo was eighteen-days-old. In order to test her motor and adaptive skills as she grew, the researchers visited her nursery on more than twenty occasions—at two-week intervals—before she reached her first birthday. She was also tested at fifteen, eighteen, and twenty-one months of age.

Gorilla babies usually begin to crawl at three months of age.

According to that study, gorilla babies learn to sit, stand, and walk twice as quickly as human babies. Although Colo's motor development was clearly accelerated compared to that of other primates, the scientists said this did not mean she had superior intellectual abilities. In fact, her quick development could prove their theory that a short period of infancy leads to a lower level of intellectual development.

The brain of a baby gorilla is about the same size as the brain of a human baby, but as time passes, the size of the human brain surpasses that of the gorilla's.

Human babies learn to crawl when they are approximately six-months-old, which is twice as long as it takes for gorilla babies.

DEVELOPMENTAL ACTIVITY	GORILLA BABIES (approximations)	HUMAN BABIES (approximations)
brings hands together in midline of body	3 weeks	2 months
gets first teeth	6 weeks	4–6 months
holds head steady and erect	12 weeks	3–5 months
sits and leans forward on hands	16 weeks	4–6 months
eats solid foods	2–3 months	4–6 months
crawls	3 months	6–8 months
walks	4–6 months	9–12 months

Willie B. was a favorite at Zoo Atlanta.

3

WILLIE B.: A STORY OF HOPE

Captured in the jungles of Africa in 1961, a three-year-old western lowland gorilla was on his way to the United States. His days of playing among the trees in Cameroon were over. Named after the then-mayor of Atlanta, William Berry Hartsfield, "Willie B." found himself in a new home: a twenty-five-by-forty-foot enclosure of concrete and glass at the Grant Park Zoo in Atlanta, Georgia.

In the early days, Willie B.'s zookeepers went into his cage to wrestle and play with him. Just as gorillas in the wild play with one another, the keepers tickled and chased him. But when they left after each play session, Willie B. tried to follow them out the door. As he grew older and stronger, the gorilla nearly tore his playmates' clothes off in an attempt to keep them from leaving. Obviously, it was no longer safe for the keepers to be inside the cage with the gorilla. From then on, the only thing Willie B. had to play with was a rubber tire hanging by a chain in the middle of his cage. And every night, when the keepers locked up the zoo, Willie B. was sent to his night pen, all alone.

Soon Willie B. grew to be a potbellied, barrel-chested, full-grown silverback gorilla. At six-feet-tall and weighing more than four hundred pounds, Willie towered over most of his keepers. His massive head sat upon his forty-inch-round neck. All day long visitors came to stare at the huge gorilla—and, unlike gorillas in the wild, Willie B. stared right back.

He passed the time people-watching. If he found visitors who particularly interested him, the great gorilla invited them to play with him. He walked toward the spectators, hitting the bars with his elbows and encouraging them to play chase.

When the visitors left each night, Willie B. gathered up any-thing he could find: sticks, rope, hair, fruit peels, pieces of tile he had removed from his cage, and sometimes bits of trash. Then the giant silverback carried his fistfuls of treasure into his night room, set them down, and fell asleep with them beside his head.

GORILLA AT A GLANCE

NAME: Willie B.

HEIGHT: 6'

WEIGHT: 450 pounds

EYE COLOR: Brown

HAIR COLOR: Black

BIRTHPLACE: Cameroon, Africa

BIRTH DATE: Sometime in 1958

FAVORITE FOODS: Melons, strawberries, grapes, and milk

FAVORITE ACTIVITIES: Splashing in the tub, swinging on a tire, people-watching

Sometimes Willie B. would offer one of these objects to a zookeeper, usu-ally as a trade for his favorite snack: fruit treats. Another favorite of Willie B.'s was his daily cup of milk. As the keepers poured the milk into a cup, Willie B. would raise his arms above his head and bark in excitement. In anticipation of the treat, the heavyweight gorilla would run around his pen, causing the walls and floor to shake!

Day after day, Willie watched the people who were watching him. He particularly liked the gum chewers, because Willie B. loved the sweet taste of gum. If he noticed someone was chewing gum, he would sit directly in front of that person. Holding a steel bar of the cage in each hand, he'd push his nose in between the bars and stare. While he stared, he pretended to be chewing gum himself. The zoo visitors often asked zookeeper Charles Horton if Willie had gum in his mouth. As soon as Charles explained that it was Willie's way of communicating that he would like some gum, the visitors almost always began to search through their pockets or purses to find a piece for Willie B. Charles always removed the wrapper and handed the gum to Willie, and then everyone watched the gum-chewing gorilla.

Although Charles never went into the cage with Willie, the two still played many games together. One activity they both enjoyed was a kind of a game of "boo." When Charles walked down the aisle between the glass and the bars, Willie would sit in the back corner of his cage, looking up and down, and acting generally uninterested. Then, once the keeper got closer, Willie B. would jump up and charge him, as silverbacks do in the wild, but in a playful way. Charles always ran away, acting more afraid than he really was. As Charles ran, he could hear Willie B. chuckling with satisfaction. Willie B. and Charles also liked to play chasing games and tug-of-war. They even pretended to wrestle by mimicking each other's actions through the glass partition.

One of Willie B.'s favorite activities was to play in a tub of water. He would hop into the tub and splash around like a little kid. With his legs hanging over one end, he would lie back, raking the water over himself. When the tile floors became wet, it was "slip-and-slide" time. Willie would run across the wet floor, plop down on his rear end, and start spinning until he crashed into the wall. Then he would get up, race to the other side of the cage, and do it all over again.

He didn't have a playmate, so Willie B. sometimes entertained himself with something as simple as a paper towel. First, he got a paper towel good and wet, and then he wrung it out. Next, he carefully straightened it, held his head up, and laid the towel across his face. He sat like that for a while, and then he wiped his face. When he finished using the towel as a washcloth, he blew his nose in it. Finally, Willie B. simply opened wide and ate his well-used (and slightly gross) paper towel!

Willie was also quite the party animal—but because he was born in the wild, his actual birthday was unknown. The zoo recorded his birthday as May 8, 1958, a combination of his estimated age (which is probably accurate to within a few months) and the date of his arrival at the zoo (May 8, 1961). Each year Willie B.'s birthday was celebrated in a big way—with free admission to the zoo and a party complete with streamers, balloons, and treats. Willie B. usually received a birthday basket filled with his favorite fruits: melons, grapes, kiwis, and strawberries. The zoo staff and visitors sang "Happy Birthday" and blew out the candles on his birthday cake. They served a bakery cake to the public and a special gorilla cake to the "birthday gorilla."

On his twenty-fifth birthday, a local company donated a colored television set, which hung from the ceiling outside his enclosure. People asked which television show Willie preferred. Did the big gorilla enjoy the drama of soap operas, the action of a football game, or a good movie? A test was set up in hopes of finding the answer. Three television sets were placed in his

Willie watches a television set outside his cage.

viewing area, each with a different channel on. Supplied with snacks, a man sat behind the middle television set observing Willie B. Instead of watching any of the shows, the gorilla simply stared at the man eating his food. Clearly Willie B. preferred people-watching—so perhaps at the zoo, *we* are the most entertaining show of all.

On another birthday, the zookeepers staged a tug-of-war with a three-inch-thick, forty-foot-long nautical rope that had once been attached to a ship's anchor. The men put a big knot in the middle of the rope so if Willie won, he wouldn't be able to pull the rope through the bars and into his cage. When the game began, five partygoers held onto one end of the rope, and Willie B. sat in his enclosure, holding onto the other. Willie held the rope effortlessly, looking rather bored. Five more men were added to the other side. Willie continued to sit as he held onto his end of the rope. Five more men joined in and grabbed hold of the rope—a grand total of fifteen men—and pulled with all their might. Well, that got Willie's attention. He stood up, let go of the rope, and sent all fifteen men flying! As the men scrambled to get back on their feet, Willie B. yanked the rope, knot and all, into his cage. He must have decided that the rope would make a fine birthday present. He held onto his new prized possession night and day for three months, playing with it during the day and coiling it up to sleep on at night.

BIG CHANGES FOR WILLIE B.

In 1984, the Grant Park Zoo, where Willie B. lived, was considered by the Humane Society of the United States to be one of the worst zoos in the country. The animals were housed in cramped, dirty, and inhumane conditions. When some animals died and some went missing, a grand jury began an investigation into the zoo. According to Former-Mayor Andrew Young, if it weren't for the zoo's star attraction—Willie B.—the whole operation might have been shut down. In 1985, Mayor Young appointed Dr. Terry Maple as the zoo's new director. Maple took charge and made some big changes, including giving the place a new name: Zoo Atlanta.

Dr. Maple knew that Willie B. drew a big crowd, but he also knew that Willie's life of solitary confinement was all wrong. "I felt sorry for Willie B.," Maple said. "He was a big, handsome fellow, and he had to be the loneliest gorilla in the world." Soon after taking the job as director, Dr. Maple took an expedition to the Congo to see how gorillas lived in the wild. He returned from Africa on a mission, eager to make changes for Willie B.'s sake.

Dr. Maple convinced a corporate sponsor to build an African rain forest at Zoo Atlanta. The new exhibit would house up to twenty-five gorillas in four areas separated by transparent walls and include an outdoor area for them. Just as in the wild, the gorillas would live in groups with one silverback, a few females, and hopefully some youngsters. On May 13, 1988, for the first time in twenty-seven years, Willie B. was ready to make his grand entrance into the outside world—in the newly finished outdoor exhibit. Zoo staff, visitors, and the media excitedly waited for the big moment when Willie B. would leave his home of concrete and bars for one of grass and sky.

Willie B. stayed in the doorway of his cage for a while, cautiously peering out. He touched the ground a few times before he gained the confidence to explore the new territory. With his friend Charles Horton close by, coaxing him and telling him not to be afraid, Willie B. took a few steps forward into the rain-forest exhibit. His head remained statue-like on his massive neck, while he looked cautiously to the right and to the left. For the first time in almost three decades, Willie B. got to see the blue sky and the green grass and to inhale a

breath of fresh, springtime air. (And, yes, gorillas do see in color.)

Shutters clicked and cameras flashed, startling the already apprehensive gorilla. Charles noticed a strong odor coming from Willie B., which a silverback emits when he is alarmed or nervous. "It's okay, Willie," Charles told him. Then the clouds opened up, and rain began to fall. When Willie B. felt the strange sensation of raindrops, he ran back to the safety of his concrete box.

Later in the day, after the press and the public had left, Charles once again coaxed Willie out into his new home. This time Willie ran to a big oak tree and snapped off one of its branches. He dashed about the habitat. Then he went to the top of the hill and looked down at all of the land around him. It seemed to the keepers that he was claiming the land as his own, posturing as male gorillas do in the wild. The echo of clanking metal doors and the hum of fluorescent lights were now a part of Willie's past.

After exploring his new land for some time, he walked down to the glass and sat, staring at his keepers. Although he was still alone, plans were being made to introduce Willie to a couple of female gorillas in the hopes that they would breed a new generation of gorillas. He had lots of land on which to roam, but he still sat by the glass most

Once Willie went outside, he dashed around his new habitat.

of the time, watching his visitors. After spending six months alone in his new habitat, the day came for Willie to meet two female gorillas, Katie and Kinyani. Their "first date" didn't go as well as some had hoped.

The smaller, but more socially experienced Katie dominated Willie from the start. She ran around the enclosure and chased him for a few laps, with Kinyani quickly joining in. In his attempt to run away, Willie stumbled and fell over backwards. Willie clearly had some lessons to learn about standing his ground—and these two females were going to teach him.

Even in his new outdoor enclosure, Willie B. spent most of his time watching people.

After Willie learned some life lessons from Katie and Kinyani, he was introduced to the gorillas who would become his lifelong mates: Choomba, Machi, Mia Moja, and Kuchi. Six years later, Willie fathered his first baby with Choomba, a female named Kudzoo. "I feel like crying," said Zoo Atlanta Director Dr. Terry Maple, watching Choomba cradle the baby she had given birth to late on a Tuesday night. Over the years, Willie B. fathered four more babies—Willie B. Jr., Olympia, Lulu, and Sukari.

Daddy Willie liked to spend time with the little ones, letting them slide down his big belly. When his mate Mia Moja became ill, Willie B. completely took over the care of their baby Olympia for a day or two. Olympia followed her big daddy around until her mother was well enough to join the troop again.

And when Willie B. Jr. fell into the moat around the gorilla enclosure, Willie B. Sr. took charge. The keepers tried to put all of the gorillas in the building so they could rescue the baby in distress without the distraction of the curious other apes, but Willie B. would not hear of it. He insisted on staying in the habitat above his

Choomba with Willie's first offspring, a female named Kudzoo

trapped little one and even helped with the rescue effort. Sure enough, Willie pulled Willie Jr. to safety. The once-lone gorilla proved to be quite the "family guy." Charles Horton says Willie has taught him a valuable lesson: "It's never too late for things to happen for you."

Willie B. enjoyed spending time with the little ones.

Sadly, in February 2000, Willie died peacefully in his sleep at the age of forty-one. Charles recalls getting an emergency call over his radio from Bernie, another of Willie's keepers. When he arrived at the gorilla house and saw Willie just lying there, Charles shook and pounded on the enormous gorilla in

hopes of reviving him. But Willie B. was gone. After a bout with pneumonia, Willie's big, old heart just gave out.

Charles could not believe it—he had just lost one of his best friends. He had cared for the gorilla almost every day for twenty-six years, and he knew Willie B. better than anyone. "Willie loved attention, and he thrived on companionship. It was a privilege to take care of Willie B. He was inventive and intelligent. He seemed to understand what you were saying. And he was playful. He was the Energizer Bunny for me," Charles said. "I always felt like he was one of my best friends. Really. Truly."

The people of Atlanta, who also loved the playful gorilla, quickly went to work on making a memorial. More than seven thousand people came to pay their respects and listen to stories about Willie B. from those who

The memorial statue in honor of Willie B., erected after his death

knew him best. Zoo Atlanta commissioned an artist to create a life-size, bronze statue of the beloved gorilla, and his ashes were secured inside. The seven-hundred-pound statue sits in the Willie B. Memorial Garden near Willie's old habitat, keeping watch over Willie's growing family.

GORILLA FACTS:
The Rest of the Story

DON'T LET THE BEDBUGS BITE!

At the end of every day, gorillas build nests to sleep in. They build new nests each night—not only because they travel within their home range to forage for food, but also because building new sleep sites helps avoid parasites that may make homes in the bedding.

© Melanie Stephens

Babies and youngsters share their mothers' nests. Four- and five-year-olds make their own nests, which are close to their mothers'. Sometimes females and young gorillas build their nests in trees.

A gorilla nest in the wild

The heavy silverback leader and most other adult males construct their nests on the ground. Once they're nestled in, gorillas sleep about nine hours a night.

Nest construction varies, but usually consists of bent or broken vines, wild grasses, and branches. Researchers can identify the size, age, activity, and organization of a gorilla troop based on the nests.

Gorillas in captivity usually build their nests on high ledges or in trees, if available. The larger gorillas make their nests on the ground. Most zoos supply their gorilla troops with nest-building materials, such as hay and wood wool (shredded trees that resemble bales of straw, only lighter in color and thicker.) At the Columbus Zoo, the silverback Mumbah likes to make his nest inside a truck tire.

LISTEN UP!

Gorillas communicate orally by using at least twenty-two distinct sounds and vocalizations. The noises they make may sound threatening, but they are simply normal parts of their speech. The apes use these sounds to identify each other, find mates, maintain relationships, and avoid and protect themselves from predators.

Gorillas sometimes "hoot" to show alarm or strength.

Gorillas may look menacing when then open their mouths wide and expose their large, scary teeth, but this is just a "happy face"—the same thing as a human smile.

And their impressive chest thumping is the gorillas' signal for excitement or alarm—the sharp, hollow sounds can be heard a nearly a mile away!

Here are some other sounds and their translations in "gorilla-speak":

YAWN = nervous
GRUNT AND ROAR = threatened
HOOT = alarmed or showing strength
BARK = curious
BELCH = feeling good

PIG-LIKE GRUNTS OR COUGH = disciplining others
HUM = enjoying good food
CHUCKLE = playful
PURR = happy, content

Gorillas also use body language. To signal various levels of aggression, a gorilla might purse his lips, walk stiff-legged, lunge, or charge. These actions are often combined with vocal cues. Here are some additional examples of body language:

STICKS OUT TONGUE = surprised or concentrating on an object
TUCKS LIP (pulls in its lip against its teeth) = hesitant, nervous, deep in thought
SLAPS OR HITS = displeasure

SITS HUNCHED OVER = submission
HUGS OR KISSES = affection, love
STARES = threatening
LOOKS DOWN = giving up

To assert authority and protect the troop, a silverback beats his chest in a nine-step ritual. He starts by hooting, then delicately places a leaf in his mouth, stands up, beats his chest, kicks out, runs sideways, tears up vegetation, then drops to all fours, and finally slaps the ground. These imposing displays are bluffs ninety-nine percent of the time—but they are usually enough to scare off predators. Even so, the silverbacks have the might to follow through if they need to!

Silverbacks assert their authority by beating their chests.

One way gorillas show affection is by hugging.

BIRD'S EYE VIEW

One of the reasons gorillas are nearing extinction is the loss of their natural habitats. People are clearing the jungles to use the wood and to create new farmland. War, poverty, remoteness, and lack of government involvement hinder conservation efforts.

In a single week in June 2004, farmers created pastures for their cattle by clearing five square miles of the mere one hundred and two square miles of mountain gorilla habitat. Because mountain gorillas have increased by fifty-six individuals

As people clear the jungle for wood and farmland, gorillas lose some of their natural habitat.

over the past ten years, the recent loss of land was considerable step backward.

But with the help of NASA (National Air and Space Administration), conservationists are using satellites to watch over some of the protected parkland inhabited by the gorillas. "Remote sensing is the only tool that we have to efficiently monitor these remote parks," says research scientist Nadine Laporte. "Satellite imagery allows park managers to update park property boundaries, map forest habitat, and look at encroachment of the park by comparing images from two different dates." This "bird's eye view" is an important tool for scientists and conservationists who, in a race against time, are working to avoid any future destruction of mountain gorilla habitat.

But lowland gorillas also need protection. Because they live in dense rain forests, researchers find it difficult to study the animals. Despite this challenge, a study of the western lowland gorilla is being conducted in a remote region in Africa's northern Congo. The research of the Mbeli Bai Gorilla Study includes social behaviors, non-vocal communication, range patterns as they relate to food sources, and DNA fingerprinting—which provides genetic descriptions of the Mbeli western lowland gorilla population.

GORILLA BUNKS

Most zoos provide their gorillas a day pen and a night pen. Having the gorillas shift back and forth makes it easier for the keepers to clean the area that the gorillas last occupied. Another reason for a "bedroom" is that, like most of us, gorillas seem to feel safer and more comfortable when sleeping in a private area where it is dark and quiet. Similar to bunk beds, the gorillas have nesting shelves up off the floor to sleep on. The gorilla troops will usually make their nests before bedding down for the night.

WHAT ARE YOU LOOKIN' AT?

Gorillas are peaceful creatures that like to mind their own business. But if a gorilla stares directly at another gorilla in the wild, this action may be taken as a threat or a challenge. However, gorillas behind glass enclosures in zoos are used to the public and usually do not feel threatened by their visitors' curious stares.

Snowflake at the Barcelona Zoo in Spain

4

SNOWFLAKE: A ONE-OF-A-KIND FIND

The African locals called him *Nfumu*, meaning "white" in their tribal language. In Spain, he was called *Copito de Nieve*, Spanish for "little snowflake." To English-speakers around the world, he was Snowflake. In any language, he was the world's one and only known albino gorilla.

Albinism is a rare genetic disorder that stops pigment-producing cells from making normal amounts of melanin—the substance that determines the color of skin, eyes, nails, beaks, feathers, and hair. The condition occurs when an animal inherits a rare recessive trait from both parents. Albino animals and humans are vulnerable to certain skin conditions and vision challenges because of their lack of pigment. In the wild, albino animals have even more to overcome. For example, a pure-white gorilla would have a hard time blending in with the jungle landscape.

More than one story has been told about the capture of Snowflake. We know for certain that on October 1, 1966, Snowflake was taken from the Rio Muni jungle in Equatorial Guinea in Africa. According to one account, African native Benito Mañé led a group of men with shotguns into the jungle. They set out to kill the gorillas that had been feasting in Benito's banana grove. When the slaughter of the entire troop of gorillas was over, the hunters discovered a white baby gorilla still clutched in his dead mother's arms. The men were amazed. Not even tribal legends had told of a white gorilla!

But the villagers tell a very different story. According to them, one day Benito Mañé and his brother set out on a trip to a nearby village to visit another brother. Benito, a farmer of the Fang tribe, carried a shotgun. When the men neared the village, a troop of gorillas attacked them. In self-defense, Benito killed the gorillas—all but one. A baby gorilla sat alone. White fur covered his pink skin, and his pale blue eyes moved back and forth, like a pendulum on a clock.

"He was totally white, without any spots, totally white—like a fresh sheet from a factory. But his eyes were like a white man's eyes, like a doll's," Benito Mañé's nephew later recalled.

No matter which story is true, the results were the same. The unusual baby gorilla lost his entire troop and became an orphan.

Benito took the little gorilla home and kept him in a cage lined with sticks, ferns, and leaves. He fed the little one meals of wild fruits and stems. After four days, he took the gorilla to the Ikunde Research Center, founded by

GORILLA AT A GLANCE

NAME: Snowflake or Copito de Nieve

TRANSLATION: "Little Snowflake" (Spanish)

HEIGHT: About 6'

WEIGHT: About 350 pounds

EYE COLOR: Blue

HAIR COLOR: White

BIRTHPLACE: Equatorial Guinea

BIRTH DATE: Sometime in 1964

FAVORITE FOODS: Bananas, raisins, and figs

FAVORITE ACTIVITIES: Posing and smiling in front of photographers, lying on his back while his keepers scratched or tickled him

the Barcelona Zoo. The white gorilla arrived coated with red road dust. After looking at his teeth, researchers determined that he was about two-years-old. He weighed nineteen pounds, ten pounds less than an average human of the same age.

Little Snowflake in Africa

Spanish naturalist Dr. Jordi Sabater Pi was working at the research center that day. He had spent his life studying and drawing gorillas, but had never seen a white one. Intrigued by this amazing discovery, he purchased the unique gorilla from Benito. About the tiny wonder, Dr. Sabater wrote, "The animal is magnificent, healthy, vivacious, but still very aggressive."

The following day, Dr. Sabater and his wife tried to give the wild gorilla a bath, but he screamed and tried to bite them. After giving the gorilla his bath, the doctor and his wife bedded him down in a cage and offered him some milk to drink. Dr. Sabater knew if the gorilla would drink the near-perfect food, his chances of surviving in captivity would increase. Snowflake drank the milk, and the slow taming process began.

By the sixteenth day, Dr. Sabater was able to touch Snowflake's head, ears, arms, and back. Soon the white gorilla was allowed to leave his cage, and he began following anyone who showed him a favorite food—bananas, sugar cane, cookies, or milk. "We worked with him for at least an hour in the morning and another hour in the afternoon," said Dr. Sabater.

At the end of the month, Snowflake was walking hand-in-hand with the people he knew well. He followed the naturalist and his wife everywhere. He also liked to play alone, clapping his hands and turning somersaults. By November 1966, the taming process was complete. The time had come to ship him to his new home—the Barcelona Zoo in Spain.

A SNOWFLAKE IN SPAIN

When Snowflake arrived, Dr. Antonio Jonch Cuspinera, the zoo director at the time, named him *Copito de Nieve*, meaning "little snowflake." Dr. Cuspinera and the zoo staff decided that the young gorilla was too small to put on display. He would need a surrogate family to raise him until he was older. The zoo's veterinarian, Dr. Roman Luera Carbo, and his wife, Maria, decided to take the little gorilla home with them.

When Snowflake arrived in Spain, he was cared for by the Barcelona Zoo's veterinarian and his wife as if he were a human baby.

Maria fed Snowflake some milk from a bottle, changed his dirty diapers, and sang him to sleep. "It was easy to forget he was a gorilla and not a human child," Maria said. The affectionate little ape demanded attention, grunted contentedly while being cuddled, and laughed delightedly when tickled. He devoured his baby food, but as he grew, his favorite foods became boiled ham, yogurt, and even cola. The little gorilla loved to play, and he got into all sorts of things. He spent hours in the backyard wrestling with and chasing the family's long-eared basset hound, Popeye.

When Snowflake misbehaved, Maria scolded him. Snowflake went into a corner, clenched his tiny fists, and whimpered. Then when Mrs. Carbo spoke, "Come here. I do love you," Snowflake came to her like a little child.

After a year of living with his surrogate family, Snowflake had grown bigger and stronger. It was time to be returned to his home at the Barcelona Zoo. Cameras rolled when he arrived, holding

When he was young, Snowflake liked to play in the yard.

onto Maria's hand. Curious locals flocked to his first public appearance, the international press came to photograph him, and the mayor stopped by for a visit. The city of Barcelona was practically giddy over the addition. After all, their zoo boasted the only albino gorilla known to man.

When the fanfare was over, Snowflake clung to his surrogate mom as she tried to peel him off her. "He got a hold of me so I wouldn't go away," Maria said. "He wanted me to stay at the zoo. It made me cry. I loved him a lot, but I knew I couldn't keep him. If only I could have kept him." That night, Maria had to turn her back and walk away from the little gorilla she had grown to love so much. Snowflake cried out, but his cries went unanswered.

Eventually he adjusted to his new home, although it had no trees to climb, no leaves to eat, and no gorilla troop to be with. He spent his days at the zoo climbing on the metal monkey bars and swinging on the ropes in his concrete enclosure. Although he was alone in a strange place, his gorilla instincts seemed to kick in. Just like his peers in the tropical rain forests, Snowflake spent his days playing, swinging, and climbing. He seemed fascinated by the water in his black rubber tub, splashing and rolling just like his wild relatives.

Snowflake climbed on the monkey bars in his new home at the zoo.

In March 1967, Snowflake—looking like a little old man with his wrinkled, pink face—appeared on the cover of *National Geographic*. He became the zoo's celebrity and one of the biggest attractions in Barcelona. But after living alone in the spotlight, he needed a companion. When Snowflake was about four-years-old, the zoo purchased a young male gorilla named Muni to be his playmate. The gorillas were about the same size and age.

Snowflake loved to splash in the water inside his rubber tub.

Although Muni was black and Snowflake was white, neither of them seemed to notice. They played the same kinds of games young gorillas like to play in the wild. Just as he did in his younger days with Popeye the dog, Snowflake liked to chase Muni and wrestle with him. When they weren't playing, they spent their time eating and sleeping.

Snowflake and Muni enjoyed wrestling.

Scientists thought it would prove interesting to go to the Barcelona Zoo to run tests on these two very different gorillas. After studying gorillas in the wild, researchers concluded that gorillas are intelligent animals that like to spend their days solving problems and making choices. To test the intelligence and resourcefulness of Snowflake and Muni, researchers hung the gorillas' favorite foods out of reach to see if they could figure out ways to get to the treats. Although Snowflake and Muni found their own solutions, Muni always solved the problems a little quicker. Muni was also the leader in the games he and Snowflake played, and he pioneered their explorations. He appeared to be the bolder one, too.

One day the researchers put a mirror in the cage. Muni immediately recognized himself and began to examine the parts of his body that he couldn't normally see. He looked under his armpits, lifted his legs, and even turned around to inspect his rear end! But when Snowflake looked into the mirror, he didn't seem to realize that he was looking at his own image. He wanted to meet the new gorilla in the cage. He searched behind the mirror, trying to find his new playmate. When he couldn't find the mystifying white gorilla, he knocked on the mirror. Frightened by his discovery, he ran from the confusing image.

The researchers noticed that Snowflake squinted, furrowed his brow, and frowned a lot, most likely to protect his eyes from bright sunlight.

When researchers put a mirror in his cage, Snowflake did not recognize himself when he looked in it.

They began to wonder if the lack of pigment in Snowflake's eyes could cause him to have poor vision. After running tests, the researchers concluded that he did have poor eyesight, which also seemed to affect his coordination and confidence.

When Snowflake and Muni grew older, they were separated to be in troops of their own. Snowflake had

Because his albinism made him more sensitive to light, Snowflake had to protect his eyes from the bright sun.

three female gorillas in his troop and eventually fathered twenty-one babies. None were albino, because both parents would have to have that recessive gene. Snowflake's babies were born during the period when zoos did not yet trust gorillas in captivity to raise their young, so all of them were raised by humans during their infancies and re-introduced into the group as youngsters.

Although Snowflake remained white throughout his life, he became a true "silverback" in his maturity—the protector and leader of his troop. Despite not being a part of a gorilla troop in his younger years, Snowflake was a gentle and able father and grandfather. The presence of the young ones—including seven young gorillas from his own line—seemed to stimulate Snowflake in his later years. He

Snowflake was a gentle father and grandfather.

became more active, and keepers noticed that he "looked happier" in his role as father, teacher, and protector of his troop.

He taught the young gorillas how to behave with the adults. At mealtime, he taught them to wait their turns, because gorilla etiquette stresses the importance of letting the silverback eat first. If the young gorillas played too roughly, he disciplined them by coughing in their faces. If they persisted, he separated them physically, but he never used too much force or aggression. Snowflake enjoyed playing with gorillas from his own line, letting them slide down his massive back and swing from his arms. During quiet times, he nuzzled their bellies with his giant muzzle. In his later years with them, Snowflake was often heard kindly grunting, purring, and rumbling.

In April 2002, an eight-month-old female from Snowflake's line, Muni, was introduced into his group. It soon became obvious that he had a "soft spot" for his youngest "grandgorilla." Snowflake was much more tolerant of her than of any of the other youngsters. He even let her steal his food!

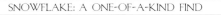

Snowflake shared a special bond with Muni, and he enjoyed living his "golden years" beside the frisky young gorilla.

By the time Snowflake neared his fortieth birthday, he had been suffering with skin cancer for three years. A biopsy had confirmed the diagnosis, and the veterinarians treated him just as they would a human with the disease. Snowflake underwent three operations to remove a tumor under his right arm. Despite all of their attempts to cure him, the lump kept growing. Eventually, it became clear that nothing else could be done.

In September 2003, the Barcelona Zoo's president announced that Snowflake was dying. City Hall removed the zoo entrance fees for children so they could come to say their last good-byes. People from Barcelona and surrounding areas flocked to the zoo to say farewell to their friend. On the first weekend after the announcement, the line was five hundred meters—more than five football fields—and two hours long. Children clung to their parents, hoping for a better view. Adults jostled each other with impatience. Everyone tried to get one last look at the white gorilla with the pink face. Upon finally seeing him, one visitor gasped, "He's gorgeous!" But Snowflake only hung his head. He sat before his many fans with his back toward them and soon lumbered off, going back the way he came, out of view of the public.

Snowflake died of skin cancer on November 24, 2003. He was thought to be between thirty-eight- and forty-years-old. Snowflake's lack of pigment made him vulnerable to the sun. In the end, what made him so unique also shortened his life. Today, four of Snowflake's twenty-one offspring still survive, plus ten of his "grandgorillas": five males and five females.

GORILLA FACTS:
The Rest of the Story

PICKY, PICKY!

An adult male gorilla spends about seven hours a day foraging or feeding, and during that day he consumes more than forty pounds of vegetation—fruits, leaves, shoots, stems, flowers, bark, seeds, and ferns.

Inside a gorilla's potbelly are very large intestines that help them digest many pounds of vegetables.

But gorillas don't eat every part of the plants. Just like someone who wants the crusts cut off his or her sandwich, these great apes are picky eaters! They may eat only the leaves, the pith (the soft, spongy center), the stalk, or the roots of a particular plant.

Most gorillas have potbellies. Inside them are super-sized intestines, which help the animals digest pound after pound of bulky vegetables and plants. When they eat fruits, gorillas disperse seeds in their dung as they move from place to place, helping new plants to sprout and grow.

Gorillas also like to grub for grubs, caterpillars, termites, ants, as well as other insects and insect larvae. Although they are not true vegetarians, about 97 percent of their diet is made of plant species—which causes them to pass gas frequently. P.U.!

What Big TEETH You Have!

All the better to eat tree bark with, my dear! The gorilla's intimidating appearance and strength have given the creature a bad rap—making hunters feel justified in slaughtering them. Some movies have also continued this mistaken stereotype, portraying gorillas as bloodthirsty, King Kong-like monsters.

Under most circumstances, gorillas have a gentle nature. Their large jaws and teeth are designed to help them eat tough bark and foliage. Their long, strong arms allow them to climb trees, where they swing and play, pick fruit and leaves to eat, build nests, and hide for safety.

Gorillas use their large jaws and teeth to eat tough bark and foliage.

Who are they hiding from? Most of the time—*us!* Humans are the number one hunter of gorillas.

Just One of the Guys

When young males, or blackbacks, mature in the wild, they may begin to challenge the dominant male, known as the silverback. When the blackbacks reach eight to twelve years of age, they become more aggressive. Suddenly the silverback is less tolerant of them.

The young males may live on the outskirts of the troop for a while before venturing off on their own. They often are driven out of the troop, pushing them to find females and start their own troops. Sometimes, male gorillas cannot find mates right away. These lone males have a tendency to form bachelor groups.

They travel in packs, trying to lure mature female gorillas from their troops to start troops of their own.

More males than females exist in captivity, so zoos are beginning to form bachelor groups. The St. Louis Zoo formed one in 1990; the Cleveland Zoo created one in 1994; and Zoo Atlanta followed in 1996. Other zoos with bachelor groups include Disney's Animal Kingdom, the Santa Barbara Zoo, the Knoxville Zoo, the Kansas City Zoo, St. Paul's Como Zoo, and the Birmingham Zoo.

Young blackbacks at the Columbus Zoo and Aquarium in Ohio

With the increasing number of captive gorilla births, zoos will need to create an additional ten to twenty bachelor groups in the next few years. Space becomes an issue with the forming of "bachelor pads." They need to be located far enough away from the troops with females so the young males are unable to pick up the scent of the females. The presence of females excites them, causing them to be more competitive and aggressive.

SENIOR GORILLAS

The estimated life span of a gorilla is up to fifty years. As of 2006, the oldest gorilla now living in captivity is Jenny at age fifty-two. Captured in the wild in 1954, she is now living at a zoo in Dallas, Texas. A gorilla named Massa at the Philadelphia Zoo was brought from the wild in 1930, and he died in 1984, making him at least fifty-four-years-old at the time of his death. Tracking the ages of gorillas in the wild is difficult, but scientists estimate that some have lived into their forties.

Koko celebrates her 30th birthday.

5

KOKO: A STORY OF FRIENDSHIP

When a baby western lowland gorilla was born on July 4, 1971, the San Francisco Zoo staff named her *Hanabi-Ko*, meaning "fireworks child" in Japanese. Her nickname became Koko.

But at the age of six months, Koko weighed only four pounds, fourteen ounces—the typical weight of a newborn gorilla. Septicemia, a disease caused by toxic organisms in the bloodstream, had spread among the gorilla population at the zoo in January 1972. The sickly infant gorilla was suffering from malnutrition and dehydration caused by the disease. Koko was near death. She was taken to the Animal Care Facility of the University of California, and the veterinarians at the medical center saved her life.

When Koko returned to the zoo, she was kept in a nursery at the Children's Zoo—away from the adult gorilla population. It was there that Koko met Penny Patterson, a young graduate student who was studying primates at nearby Stanford University. Because of her lifelong love of animals, Penny decided to devote her studies to the language abilities of animals. Penny visited the little gorilla every day in the hopes of teaching her sign language. Project Koko had begun.

During their first visit on July 12, 1972, Koko—who now weighed twenty pounds and was a little more than a year old—sat on the nursery floor. Penny signed, "Hello" (a gesture somewhat like a salute). Koko put her hand on Penny's head and patted it. When Penny sat down, the gorilla pulled on Penny's hair. Koko bit her new visitor at times, but other times chose to ignore her altogether. Their difficult relationship continued for a while, and although Koko didn't seem to like her uninvited guest, Penny did not give up. She kept visiting, day after day.

After a while, Koko began to trust her persistent new friend. Once Penny had earned Koko's trust, she started taking the little gorilla for daily piggy-back-style walks around the zoo to visit the

GORILLA AT A GLANCE

NAME: Hanabi-Ko

TRANSLATION: "Fireworks Child" (Japanese)

NICKNAME: Koko

HEIGHT: 5' 3/4"

WEIGHT: 280 pounds

EYE COLOR: Dark brown

HAIR COLOR: Black to dark brown

BIRTHPLACE: San Francisco Zoo, California

BIRTH DATE: July 4, 1971

FAVORITE FOODS: Nuts, tofu dishes, apples, and corn on the cob

FAVORITE ACTIVITIES: Playing with dolls, playing chase, drawing, writing, and watching movies

other animals. Penny liked to play little games with Koko. She breathed fog onto the glass of the large windows in the nursery and then drew stars and simple faces on the misted surface. Koko loved the game, and she drew, too.

Penny used "total communication" with Koko, which means she said a word aloud as she signed it to Koko. At first, she taught Koko three words: "drink," "food," and "more." One month after the lessons had begun, Koko put her hand to her mouth and made the sign for food. Penny couldn't believe

When she was about one-year-old, Koko began to learn sign language from Penny Patterson.

her eyes—Koko had communicated with her for the first time using sign language! Koko seemed to sense how happy her teacher was. She grabbed a bucket, plunked it over her head, and ran wildly around the playroom.

By age two, Koko was stringing words together to form sentences. Just like humans, Koko found it easier to learn words for objects (nouns) than to learn action words (verbs).

"There mouth, mouth you there," Koko signed when she wanted Penny to make fog on the nursery window so they could draw in it with their fingers. When she was thirsty, Koko signed, "Pour that hurry drink hurry," and when she was hungry, "More, eat."

When Koko was three-years-old, she moved from the Children's Zoo to Stanford University, where Penny Patterson was studying. Penny hoped that the new location would help Koko concentrate on her language lessons without any distractions. At first, Koko made angry display charges at the door of her enclosure. "Go home," she

Penny and Koko spent time at Stanford University in California practicing language lessons.

signed, wanting to get out. Penny stayed with her every night as Koko cried in her sleep, "Whoo-whoo, whoo-whoo." It took some time, but eventually Koko accepted that she was in her new home.

Penny tried to comfort Koko by reading lots of picture books to her. Like most toddlers, Koko loved story time. Sometimes she took a book off on her own and studied the pictures and signed to herself. Her favorite books were about gorillas, but she also loved books about cats. She chose the story "Puss in Boots" quite often, but her all-time favorite was "The Three Little Kittens." Whenever she got to the page where the mother was angry and the kittens were crying, Koko would sign, "Mad."

By the time she was five-years-old, Koko knew more than two hundred words. That's about the same number of words a two-and-a-half-year-old human boy or girl knows. When Koko was asked if she was an animal or a person, she signed, "Fine animal gorilla."

Every year, Penny celebrated Koko's birthday with cake, sparkling cider, and lots of presents. Koko seemed to understand birthdays. When asked what she does on hers, Koko answered, "Eat, drink, old." Three days before Koko's twelfth birthday, Patterson asked her what she wanted for a gift. Koko signed, "Cat, cat, cat." Penny didn't want to give Koko a stuffed cat because she knew she would destroy it. In a mail-order catalog, she found a cement cat statue covered with vinyl and black velvet. She ordered the gift, but the shipment didn't come until after Koko's birthday. Penny decided to wait and give the gift to Koko on the following Christmas.

On December 25, 1983, Penny anxiously waited for Koko to open her gift, expecting her to love it. But Koko looked at the black cat statue and signed, "Red," which is the word she often signed when she was angry. Then she charged about the room, banging on the walls. At first, Penny was confused by Koko's display of anger. She began to wonder if Koko was upset because she had hoped for a live cat. Maybe Koko wanted a pet.

Six months later, Penny's assistant, Karen, found a litter of orphaned kittens. The two women decided that when the kittens were old enough, they would bring the litter in and allow Koko to choose a pet. When that day came, Karen arrived with three kittens and showed them to Koko. "Love

Penny Patterson gave Koko a kitten after Koko signed that she wanted a cat for her birthday present.

that," Koko signed. One by one, she blew in the kitten's faces, giving each one the same "blow test" she gives all new animals or people she met. Koko pointed to the tailless gray tabby. "That," she signed. Penny never asked Koko why she chose the tabby, but she wondered if it was because he had no tail, since a gorilla has no tail.

The very first time Koko picked up the male tabby, she sat down and tried to tuck him in her thigh. That's where mother gorillas put their babies. Then she placed the tiny

Koko tried to tuck her kitten in her thigh, much like this gorilla mother does with her baby.

kitten on her massive stomach and gently stroked him. She signed to Penny, "Love soft cat." Penny asked Koko what she would name the kitten, and Koko signed, "All Ball." Penny agreed that this would be a good name, since without a tail the kitten looked like a ball of fur.

Koko treated Ball as if he were her baby. She held the kitten in her arms, petting it softly while it purred. "Baby," Koko signed. She cradled the tabby in her legs and examined its paws. Koko squeezed gently, and the kitten's claws came out. "Cat do scratch," Koko signed. "Koko love."

As Ball grew older, Koko carried him on her back, just as mother gorillas carry their young. She liked to play chase with the kitten and tickle him. At first, Penny worried about leaving the kitten unsupervised with Koko, but the kitten sneaked into Koko's enclosure anyway. Koko was always gentle, and Ball was never afraid of her. Whenever Koko signed about Ball, she always used the word "love."

On a foggy December morning, Ball died suddenly. Penny went to see Koko and signed to her in American Sign Language. She told Koko that All Ball had died. The gorilla sat in silence. Penny left wondering if Koko understood what she had said. Ten minutes later, she heard a loud, long series of high-pitched hoots, sounding like, "Whoo-whoo, whoo-whoo." It was the unmistakable sound of a gorilla crying. Penny cried, too.

A few days later, she had a conversation with Koko about Ball. "Do you want to talk about your kitty?" she signed.

Koko signed, "Cry."

"Can you tell me more about it?" Penny asked.

"Blind," she signed.

"We don't see him anymore, do we? What happened to your kitty?"

"Sleep cat," Koko signed.

"How did you feel when Ball died?"

Koko signed, "Cry sad frown."

News of All Ball's death traveled quickly. Television stations and newspapers across the country told the story of the gorilla whose pet kitten had died. People of all ages sent cards and letters expressing their sympathy to Koko. Some people shared stories with Koko about losing their own pets. Many children sent photographs of their cats, and some drew pictures for Koko. Penny and Koko looked through the cards and letters together. They all had the same message—that Koko should get a new kitten. In January, Penny showed Koko a picture of three cat drawings. One had a long tail, one had a short tail, and one was tailless. "When you get another kitty, which one do you want?" Penny signed as she spoke the words aloud.

"That," Koko signed, pointing to the tailless kitten.

"We'll get you a kitty like that," Penny said. "Is that okay?"

"Good. Nice," Koko signed.

The search was on. Penny learned of a tailless breed of cat called a Manx, but it wasn't until March that Penny found a red, tiger-striped one. Penny knew that red was Koko's favorite color. When Koko saw the kitten, the gorilla purred with pleasure. She placed him on her chest and petted him.

Penny gave Koko a Manx kitten, a tailless breed of cat, like the one above.

"Let me hold the kitty," Penny said. But Koko would not let go. She kissed her kitten, then wrapped both arms around it and looked down at it lovingly. She signed, "Love that baby."

"Koko uses sign language to rhyme, to joke, and even to tell lies," says Penny. One time Koko was caught chewing on a crayon when she was supposed to be drawing.

"You're not eating that, are you?" Penny asked.

She quickly took the crayon out of her mouth and moved it across her lips as if she were putting on lipstick. "Lip," Koko signed.

"My life with Koko is full of surprises, and sometimes frustration, for even though Koko is very lovable, she can be a stubborn gorilla. I will never stop teaching Koko, and in her own way, she will never stop teaching me."

Today, Koko "communicates" with the world about the plight of her relatives in the wild. On July 28, 2005, wildlife conservationist, Aleisha Caruso conveyed Koko's message through an interactive multimedia workshop entitled "Meet Koko—Ambassador for Endangered Species" at the Children's World Summit for the Environment in Aichi, Japan. More than one thousand school children from 150 countries attended the summit in Aichi to discuss their concerns about environmental issues and the future of their planet. Koko's message urged the new generation of world leaders to help protect a species in danger of extinction.

Koko also "communicates" over the Internet to convey her messages of conservation and survival of the species. Recently, more than 20,000 people logged on to one of her online chats.

GORILLA FACTS:
The Rest of the Story

GORILLA TALK

For many years, scientists have wondered why apes, though clearly intelligent, cannot learn to speak like humans. Efforts to teach them how to formulate words have always failed. Gradually it became clear that apes lack the muscles that we humans use to control our voices. Besides that, the tongues of apes are very long and are not shaped to form words. However, scientists have known that gorillas communicate with each other through gestures.

American Sign Language—or "Amesan" as it is called by the deaf community—is used by more than three hundred thousand deaf or mute Americans. ASL is not "finger spelling" of the alphabet. It would take too long to communicate that way. Instead, ASL takes shortcuts. Movements made with the face, hands, arms, and body can all be signs for complete words or ideas. Sign language leaves out unnecessary words.

CAT

RED   DRINK

HUNGRY

IF YOU'RE HAPPY AND YOU KNOW IT . . .

Happy gorillas sing. Biologist Ian Redmond reports that they make a certain sound, something between a dog whining and a person singing, when they are especially happy. On a sunny day when foraging is particularly good, the troop will eat, "sing," and put their arms around each other.

HAUNTINGLY HUMAN

Gorilla keeper Dan Nellis of the Columbus Zoo in Ohio says, "Gorillas are hauntingly human. I communicate with them with body language and eye contact. They know all of their keepers individually. Once you get to know them, they are so much like us it's unbelievable. Anakka, a four-hundred-pound silverback gorilla, can do the Hokey-Pokey."

Fubo, a silverback that resides in the Bronx Zoo in New York, likes to play "scary gorilla" with his keepers. He hides his massive body behind a large rock until he spies a zookeeper walking down the steps. Then Fubo jumps out with his arms outstretched. *Boo!* When the keeper jumps in fright, the giant gorilla puts his hand over his mouth and chuckles.

CAN ANIMALS CRY?

In researching his book *The Expression of the Emotions in Man and Animals*, published in 1872, scientist Charles Darwin looked for evidence that animals did or did not shed tears. Sir E. Tennant reported to Darwin that newly captured Indian elephants in Sri Lanka that were tied up "showed no other indication of suffering other than the tears, which suffused their eyes and flowed incessantly." Another captured elephant separated from his family, when bound, sank to to ground, "uttering choking cries, with tears trickling down his cheeks." Elephant hunters told tales of elephants having large tears stream from their eyes after they were shot. Elephant zookeepers have also reported seeing elephants shed tears when family members are removed from the enclosure.

Poodles have reportedly shed tears when left behind by their owners.

Elephants are not the only animals that have been observed crying emotional tears. Biochemist William Frey, who studies human emotional tears, has received reports of dogs—particularly poodles—shedding tears in emotional situations, such as when they are left behind by their owners. There have also been reports of giraffes shedding tears when separated from their companions, trapped beavers crying when caught in traps, and adult seals crying as they watched young seal pups being killed by hunters.

Usually gorillas express their crying with mournful sounds and not tears. But there is a single account of a gorilla shedding tears. Dian Fossey told of Coco, a female mountain gorilla who was three- or four-years-old when her troop was killed before her eyes in order to secure

Adult seals have also reportedly cried emotional tears.

her capture. Coco spent the next month in a tiny cage and was very ill when Fossey rescued her and released the gorilla into an indoor pen with windows. When Coco first looked out the window of her pen at a forested mountainside like the one she grew up in, she suddenly began "to sob and shed actual tears."

Bongo, Bridgette, and Fossey at the Columbus Zoo and Aquarium in Ohio

6

BONGO AND BRIDGETTE
A STORY OF LOVE AND LOSS

Tension filled the ape house at the Columbus Zoo in Ohio. Bongo, the huge, four-hundred-fifty-pound gorilla, had been throwing feces at his keepers and his visitors. He treated Colo, his mate of twenty-five years, roughly, forcing her to give up her share of food at feeding time. Bongo would sit for hours, just staring at the concrete walls that held him captive.

In the 1970s and early 1980s, the care of gorillas involved merely keeping their cages clean and feeding them twice a day. They lived in stark concrete and steel cages and were on constant display with no privacy and no place to hide. When the gorilla mothers gave birth, the standard procedure at most zoos was to take the babies and have humans raise them in nurseries. The conditions seemed to bother Bongo.

The keepers at the Columbus Zoo sensed that the care their gorillas were receiving was inadequate. Keeper Beth Armstrong looked at Bongo and said, "This is absolutely wrong." She lay awake at night thinking of ways to change things. Beth channeled her frustrations about Bongo into a positive thing. She and fellow keepers Dianna Frisch and Charlene Jendry networked with several zoos in the Netherlands and England to improve the lives of gorillas in captivity.

Then, in 1983, a visitor came to the zoo, and she helped the keepers make more key changes.

When the visitor entered the ape house, Bongo was lying down in his cage with his back to the entrance. She walked to the opposite side of the cage, bent down, not quite kneeling, and began talking to the silverback in a "gorilla language" she had learned when she had spent more than a decade living among troops of wild mountain gorillas in Central Africa. Bongo moved closer to the woman. Soon they were nose to nose, communicating with each other. The visitor was researcher Dian Fossey. Dian was so impressed with the magnificent silverback that she extended her stay to work with the keepers and share her knowledge of how gorillas lived in the wild.

GORILLA AT A GLANCE

NAME: Bongo

HEIGHT: 6'

WEIGHT: 450 pounds

EYE COLOR: Rust brown

HAIR COLOR: Black, silver back, reddish brown on top of head

BIRTHPLACE: (Formerly) Victoria, Cameroon, Africa

BIRTH DATE: Sometime in 1956 or 1957

FAVORITE FOODS: Grapes, oranges, and most other fruits

FAVORITE ACTIVITIES: Running with the keepers, playing "chase me," playing tug-of-war and follow-the-leader with Fossey

After Dian's visit, the keepers and the staff at the Columbus Zoo decided to separate Bongo and Colo to see if Bongo's behavior would improve. They put him in an enclosure with an indoor and outdoor area, so he could spend time away from the public.

Bongo became more playful and active in his private enclosure, but he called to Colo constantly. Colo seemed more content without Bongo pushing her around, so the keepers introduced him to several other female gorillas to take his mind off Colo. But the twenty-eight-year-old silverback seemed uninterested—that is, until April 1985, when he met a twenty-five-year-old, slightly overweight gorilla named Bridgette.

From the beginning, the relationship between Bridgette and Bongo was special. Maybe Bridgette found Bongo's confident manner irresistible. She followed him around, wanting to be close to him. Bongo finally seemed relaxed, content, and happy. He spent his time tickling and teasing Bridgette, and her deep, throaty gorilla chuckles filled the ape house. They seemed to be the perfect match.

A little more than a year later, on August 13, 1986, at 10:00 P.M., Bongo

At the Columbus Zoo, Jack Hanna holds J. J., a gorilla that was named after him.

GREAT APE!

Bongo was a four-hundred-fifty-pound gorilla on a six-foot frame with a beautiful tapered coat covering his muscular body. Zookeeper Beth Armstrong said, "Bongo was an exceptionally handsome gorilla—he had sheer physical beauty. His heavily lined face and perfectly proportioned body were extraordinary."

Jack Hanna, Director of the Columbus Zoo from 1978 to 1992 and current Director Emeritus, said of the gorilla, "Bongo was a tremendous creature—he had all the fierce qualities necessary for a dominant silverback, yet all the gentleness of a kitten when around the gorilla babies."

became the oldest gorilla dad in captivity. The thirty-year-old silverback sat quietly in the cage while Bridgette gave birth to a four-pound male. For the first time, Bongo was allowed to stay in the cage with his mate during and after the birth. Due to a lack of understanding, the keepers believed that Bongo's former mate, nursery-raised Colo, did not have the maternal instincts needed to raise her young. All of Colo and Bongo's babies were taken from them to be raised by humans. However, both

GORILLA AT A GLANCE

NAME: Bridgette

HEIGHT: Less than 5'

WEIGHT: 264 pounds

EYE COLOR: Brown

HAIR COLOR: Brown and black

BIRTHPLACE: West Africa

BIRTH DATE: Sometime in 1961

FAVORITE FOODS: "Everything"

FAVORITE ACTIVITIES: Napping and eating

Bongo and Bridgette were born in the wild, so the zoo staff hoped they had learned from their parents how to care for their young. Finally, Bongo would be given the opportunity to help raise his own baby.

As Bridgette cleaned the newborn baby, she examined each of his fingers and toes. His skin had a healthy, pink glow, but he didn't seem to have as much hair as most newborns. Bongo watched quietly from the corner of the cage. After a while, he went over and sat close to Bridgette, hesitantly reaching out to touch the baby. Bridgette calmly pushed his hand away, letting him know that she was in charge. Although silverbacks lead and defend the troop, it is the females' job to raise the babies.

Bongo pulled his hand back and scratched his eyebrow. On his next attempt, he seemed to try to fool Bridgette. He turned away and rolled his eyes upward, pretending not to be looking while he reached out to touch the baby. But Bridgette was not to be tricked. She nudged his hand away from the infant gorilla.

A discouraged Bongo put his huge fingers to his mouth, chewing on them in apparent frustration. Slowly, he tried again, but she gently pushed him away. Then, as if unable to control his urges, Bongo bit down on his huge knuckles. Seemingly respecting his mate's wishes, he sat by her side while she fed the baby during the night.

Bridgette and baby Fossey

By the following day, Bridgette finally relaxed enough to let Bongo stroke the tiny baby. Bongo, so powerful that he could win a tug-of-war against six grown men, was a gentle dad. The keepers named the baby Fossey, in honor of the famous field researcher who shared their love of gorillas.

One day, when Bridgette ventured to an outdoor cage to forage, the sleeping baby Fossey woke up. Bongo heard the baby stirring in his nest. He looked for his mate, but she was nowhere in sight. Soon the baby's stirring turned to cries. Bongo looked back at the nest and again looked around for his mate. When he realized Bridgette couldn't hear the baby, he scooped Fossey up in an armful of hay and cradled the tiny gorilla in his enormous hands.

Although Bongo had his tender moments, he also loved to play. One of his favorite games was throwing a ball in the air and catching it without looking. After catching the ball, he would look over his shoulder at his keepers and make a noise that sounded like "hmph." He also liked to play a version of "Chase Me." Racing up and down his cage floor, Bongo tried to beat his keeper to the other side. When the keeper caught up with him, Bongo rolled away and ran to the other side, only to begin all over again.

Bongo and Bridgette liked to play, too. One afternoon as Bongo leaned up against the mesh of his cage and Bridgette sat on a tire with her baby close by, Bongo tossed a yellow ball in the air. Bridgette tried to knock it away. Bongo caught the ball, looked at it, and then looked at Bridgette. With thoughtful intention, Bongo gently tossed the ball at her head. As Bridgette fell backwards, she tossed her arms about playfully. When she got up, both gorillas shared in gorilla laughter.

Bongo, Bridgette, and Fossey were a happy family.

Bridgette, Bongo, and Fossey were tight-knit. As Fossey grew, he liked jumping on his tolerant father and pulling on his arms and legs. Bongo tickled Fossey and wrestled with him. They liked to play chase, with Bongo leading and looking back over his shoulder at Fossey. Another pastime was playing games of tug-of-war. The mighty Bongo pretended to struggle with the rope against the young Fossey.

Sadly, the trio enjoyed being together for only a short time. Soon after Fossey's first birthday, Bridgette became ill. The keepers separated Bongo and

Bridgette so she could rest. Bongo seemed to sense that something was wrong, but he remained unruffled. The baby was able to visit both parents through a small door between the two cages. As young gorillas do, Fossey spent most of his time with his mother.

As Bridgette's illness progressed, she stopped eating. One day when Fossey tried to nurse, she pushed him away. Baby Fossey jumped on his mother's back and cried out, but she ignored his repeated cries. Dejected, he quietly got off her back and went to sit by his father's side in the adjacent cage.

Bridgette died on October 7, 1987, from an infection associated with diverticulitis, an intestinal condition. Bongo called to his mate as they took her body away. For three long days, Bongo sat slumped against the back door, and Fossey leaned against him. Their mournful cries filled the gorilla house.

Although the females usually provide most of the care of the youngsters, the keepers had faith that Bongo would take good care of Fossey. Bongo did not disappoint them. Every night, Bongo gathered hay and made Fossey's nest—right next to his. At eating time, Bongo saved large portions of his food for Fossey, who ate his choice of foods while leaning up against his dad. The keepers actually began to worry whether Bongo was getting enough to eat!

After Bridgette passed away, Bongo and Fossey became inseparable.

The two became inseparable and spent hours playing together. Bongo put his huge mouth over Fossey, tickling him like a mother who blows on her baby's belly. When Fossey ran off to play outdoors with another young gorilla, Bongo kept watch nearby. In time, Fossey's physical movements began to mirror those of his father.

"Fossey was a very secure and self-confident gorilla, almost to the point of being cocky," keeper Dianna Frisch said. "He knew his dad was right there to back him up."

Bongo's first parental crisis came when Fossey was sick with flu-like symptoms. For two days, the silverback cupped the little one in his massive hands, making soothing sounds and stroking the shivering baby until he was well again.

When the local media heard about how the gorilla dad had adjusted so well to single fatherhood, they wrote an article about him, declaring Bongo, "Father of the Year." After about a year, the zookeepers introduced Bongo and Fossey to a thirteen-year-old female named Molly. Molly began caring for little Fossey almost immediately. Only a few hours after the introduction, a keeper watched as Molly looked Fossey over and washed his ears in a motherly fashion.

Zookeepers introduced Molly as a surrogate mom to Fossey.

Bongo enjoyed his new group for several months. Then, on the morning of September 25, 1990, zookeeper Beth Armstrong found Bongo slumped over in his cage with Molly standing over his body. Four-year-old Fossey stood, bending over Bongo and trying to look into his father's unseeing eyes. Bongo had died in his sleep of an apparent heart attack at the age of thirty-four.

Bongo's majestic dignity and Bridgette's gentleness live on in Fossey, who now resides at a zoo in Little Rock, Arkansas.

GORILLA FACTS:
The Rest of the Story

EXTRA! EXTRA! GORILLA NEWS

Bongo's story helped bring the world's gorilla-keeper community together. The efforts of the staff at the Columbus Zoo to seek opinions of their peers at other zoos led to improving the lives of captive gorillas. The networking led to the founding of the *Gorilla Gazette*, a periodical in which the keepers share new ideas and stories. The Columbus Zoo keepers created and published the *Gorilla Gazette* publication from 1987 through December 2000 with more than twenty-five issues. Today, Gorilla Haven in Georgia publishes the *Gorilla Gazette*, with Beth Armstrong as a coeditor.

Their networking also inspired the first gorilla workshop, held in Columbus in June 1990. The gathering of gorilla experts gave the keepers an opportunity to listen to presentations, learn about conservation, and share stories and research about gorilla behavior, diet, births, and deaths. These workshops continue to this day, hosted by different zoos.

BABYING BABY

Baby gorillas have a white tail tuft. This may help the mother locate her baby in the jungle. As long as the baby has that white hair, every member of the troop usually gives it special treatment. The troop members seem to be more forgiving and lenient with the white-tufted babies. After the baby loses the white hair, it must follow the troop's rules.

A baby gorilla that has a white tail tuft (shown here) receives special treatment from other members of the troop.

NO ONE LOVED GORILLAS MORE

Dr. Dian Fossey (1932–1985) was one of the world's best-known gorilla researchers. She lived among the wild mountain gorilla troops in Africa.

"I shall never forget my first encounter with gorillas," she said. "Sound preceded sight. Odor preceded sound in the form of an overwhelming musky, barnyard, humanlike scent."

Dr. Dian Fossey knuckle-walking with her gorilla friends in central Africa

Dr. Fossey spent sixteen years living among the wild mountain gorilla troops, winning their trust by imitating them—feeding, scratching, and vocalizing. Her actions seemed to relax the gorillas and arouse their curiosity. Because standing upright increased the gorillas' apprehension, she spent her days knuckle-walking among her gorilla friends.

In 1980, Dian Fossey returned to America for three years to teach at Cornell University, give lectures, and promote her new book, *Gorillas in the Mist*. While she traveled the country, she also educated zookeepers about a gorilla's physical, psychological, and social needs. She stressed that gorillas should have trees to climb on and sleep in, and she encouraged the keepers to supply hay or some type of bedding so the gorillas could build nests as they do in the wild. Since gorillas spend most of their days foraging for food, Fossey recommended that the keepers cut the food in small pieces and hide them among the hay and trees. She also taught the keepers about proper social structure within gorilla troops, stressing the need for mother-reared infants and a variety of ages within each gorilla troop.

Although she became a hero to gorillas in captivity, Dian Fossey began as a self-appointed protector of gorillas in the wild. She waged war against anyone or anything that posed a threat to them, fighting for the gorillas as if her own survival depended on it. By forming anti-poaching patrols and enforc-ing park borders, she saved some gorillas and their habitats from destruction.

Protecting gorillas is what she lived for—and in the end, it was what she died for. In the early-morning hours of Thursday, December 27, 1985, Dian Fossey was found murdered in her cabin on the mountain in Central Africa. To this day, the crime remains unsolved. She was buried in Rwanda in a gravesite that she herself had constructed for her dead gorilla friends. As it says on her tombstone, no one loved gorillas more.

"Nyiramachabelli"
(The Woman Who Lives Alone on the Mountain)
Dian Fossey
1932–1985

No one loved gorillas more
Rest in peace, dear friend
Eternally protected
In this sacred ground
For you are home
Where you belong

BABY LOVE AND BASIC GROOMING

A baby gorilla usually feeds on its mother's milk until it is about two-years-old. As the baby grows, its fingernails do, too. Sometimes the little one's nails dig into its mom's flesh as it nurses, causing the mom discomfort. A mother gorilla trims her baby's fingernails by gently using her teeth. After trimming the nails, she rubs them against her chest to check for ragged edges.

A gorilla mother grooms her young.

At three to six months, the baby begins to eat solid food, but only after the mother first chews the vegetables and fruits. A mother and a baby gorilla usually have a very close and special bond. The little one stays close to its mother, sleeping in her nest, until it is four- or five-years-old.

PLAYTIME

Just like people, gorillas play to build their strength and to learn how to get along with others. Young gorillas in the wild spend their days climbing trees, swinging on vines, and playing tag. They somersault, slide, and act silly by putting twigs and leaves on their heads and running around. They play games very similar to children's games, such as king of the mountain, follow-the-leader, and even catch with large round fruit.

Young gorillas in captivity swing on ropes and climb fake trees, if provided. They have also been seen playing a game in which they put their hands over their eyes and spin around and around. When they stop spinning, they fall down and bump into things and break out in gorilla laughter.

Sometimes the little ones imitate the silverbacks by doing "bluff charges." A silverback may beat its chest and charge to show its dominance. The babies copy the big daddies by beating their chests or bellies as if to say, "I'm strong!" Little gorillas in the wild and in captivity seem to enjoy splashing and playing in the water. They also like to climb on a huge silverback as if a he's a living jungle gym!

Adult gorillas are generally less active. They like to sit back and watch the little ones chase each other, but sometimes they become part of the game. Having the little ones around seems to make the older gorillas more active and more content.

Young gorillas playing on a rope swing

Dotty Mashavu at the Columbus Zoo and Aquarium in Ohio

7

DOTTY MASHAVU
AN ADOPTION STORY

In the middle of the night on April 17, 2004, eleven-year-old Nia paced the floor of her cage. Occasionally she stopped to make nests out of bundles of hay. Then she rolled around the floor of her pen in obvious distress. The mood among her western lowland gorilla family grew quiet. Whenever Nia rested, her mom, Sylvia; brother, Little Joe; and younger sister, Mo'Ana, all sat beside her. The silverback, Mac, sat alone, keeping a distant eye on the troop.

About nine hours later, Nia climbed up into one of the nests in a chute at the back of the cage and silently gave birth to her first baby. One by one, Nia's mother and siblings came to look at the newest member of their family. Little Joe seemed to stare in amazement. The baby gorilla with extremely plump cheeks weighed about four pounds. The keepers at Ohio's Columbus Zoo named her "Dotty *Mashavu*." (*Mashavu* means "chubby cheeks" in Swahili.)

Unfortunately, things were not going well within the troop at the time of Dotty's birth. Dotty's grandmother, Sylvia, was in the final stages of cancer, and she had trouble caring for three-year-old Mo'Ana. Nia tried to care for her newborn baby and her sister, but she didn't get much sleep and soon developed a fever.

Zookeepers became alarmed when Nia started leaving Dotty in her nest for long periods of time. Mother gorillas usually stay with their babies day and night. During the day, the baby hangs onto its mother's belly or back by locking its toes into the mother's hair. At night, the mother and baby sleep together in the nest up until the youngster is four- or five-years old.

"The most natural thing for a baby gorilla is to be held by its mother," says keeper Barbara Jones. "It gives them security, and it gives them confidence." With no mother to hold onto, Dotty lay alone in her nest, hugging herself and locking her toes.

GORILLA AT A GLANCE

NAME: Dotty Mashavu

TRANSLATION: "Chubby Cheeks" (Swahili)

HEIGHT: 36"

WEIGHT: 38 pounds

EYE COLOR: Brown

HAIR COLOR: Brown and black

BIRTHPLACE: Columbus Zoo, Columbus, Ohio

BIRTH DATE: April 17, 2004

FAVORITE FOODS: Anything Mumbah is eating, grapes, Jell-O, and cooked apples

FAVORITE ACTIVITIES: Swinging from the ceiling and taking piggyback rides

The keepers spent the first few weeks trying to get Nia to care for her baby, but Dotty kept losing weight. They even tried separating Nia and her baby from the rest of the troop. Mac showed his anger at this by coughing angrily at the keepers. He sat strategically in the doorways, trying to prevent any further separation of his troop. "It was hard not to take it to heart," says zookeeper Dan Nellis, "because I felt like he was blaming me."

Even apart from the others, Nia continued to treat Dotty as if she were a doll, not a baby. She didn't feed her regularly, and she left her alone in the nest

Dotty's birth mother, Nia

for long periods of time. Dotty continued to hug herself and lock her toes together, both signs of stress. The keepers monitored her and discovered that she was still losing weight. Dotty was three-weeks-old when the zoo staff decided to take her out of the exhibit for her own survival.

It was 2004, forty-eight years since the first gorilla had been born in captivity. Over the years the keepers had learned that the longer babies stayed in the nursery, the harder it was to convince them that they were gorillas, not humans. They also knew that the baby and its adoptive gorilla troop needed to see, touch, hear, and smell each other in order for the adoption process to be successful. So, instead of rearing her in a nursery built for humans, keepers raised Dotty in an exhibit beside a gorilla troop. Led by a silverback named Mumbah, the troop included three females, Pongi, Cassie, and Jumoke, and two young males, Jontu and Muchana, born to Jumoke.

The zookeepers would need to provide Dotty with foster care until the new gorilla troop showed signs of accepting her. With an army of eight keepers, they cared for the infant in eight-hour shifts, twenty-four hours a day. With no gorilla mom to care for Dotty, the keepers at the zoo mimicked the actions of a gorilla mother. They paced the cage on all fours with baby Dotty clinging

One way keepers mimicked the actions of a gorilla mother was pacing the floor with Dotty on their backs.

to their backs. At feeding time, they grunted as they shared food with the baby on their chests. After lunch they rolled around with the little one, tickling and play-biting. If she misbehaved, they pushed her to the ground and coughed in her face. When the day was done, they slept with the tiny gorilla, holding her close through the night.

"People can mimic gorilla behavior, but the best way for a gorilla to learn social behavior is from other gorillas," says anthropologist and zookeeper Beth Armstrong. "The life of a gorilla family centers around its babies. The infant learns from the adults in the group. With a baby present, the juveniles learn how to behave with younger ones. It's important for gorillas to have age diversity in their group since they all learn from each other."

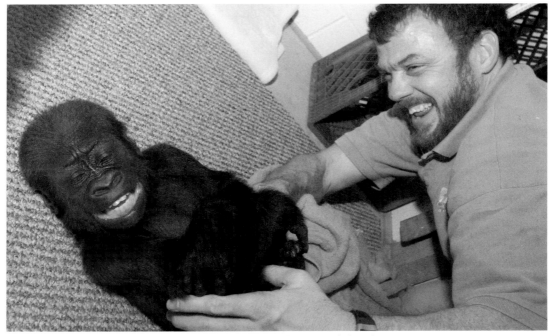

To simulate gorilla behavior, keepers tickled Dotty like other members of her troop might have done.

The oldest female in Dotty's new troop, forty-one-year-old Pongi, quickly showed an interest in Dotty. She sat beside the young gorilla most of the day, petting her and kissing her through the mesh door. Pongi spent the rest of her day warming up to Mumbah, hoping the silverback would welcome the new baby into their group. She sat beside him, touching him gently. Eventually Mumbah seemed to give in, and he sat by little Dotty at the mesh door, too. He made soft noises, showing his acceptance of the new baby.

Finally, after six months of being neighbors, Pongi was released into Dotty's cage. When the full-grown gorilla entered, Dotty clung to the bars of the cage, keeping a close eye on her human keepers. She watched as Pongi dug through the hay, discovering pieces of popcorn and fruit. For a half an hour more, Pongi

It didn't take long for Dotty and her surrogate mom, Pongi, to bond.

acted as if she was more interested in foraging for food than in approaching the infant gorilla. The keepers were proud of Pongi. They believed she acted in this manner purposely so she wouldn't scare Dotty. When Pongi sensed that the baby was comfortable with her, she scooped Dotty into her arms, making comforting noises. After a while Pongi set her down and followed her around. When Dotty climbed too high on the bars, Pongi hooted to her, coaxing her to come down from her dangerous perch.

One day not long after, keeper Barbara Jones noticed Dotty was making choking noises. She rushed into the section of the exhibit that only the baby gorilla could enter. She reached out to Dotty, but the baby gorilla ran from Barbara—and into Pongi's arms. Thankfully it turned out that Dotty wasn't choking after all, but her preference for the mother gorilla over a human assured Barbara that the adoption was a success.

Dotty playing outside in the yard

Pongi and Dotty were allowed to bond for a couple of weeks before Mumbah, the silverback, joined the new group. Eight months later, two more females were added back to the troop: sixteen-year-old Jumoke and twelve-year-old Cassie. These two younger females helped take some of the parenting burden from Pongi and Mumbah, who were both in their forties. Cassie was so excited when she first saw Dotty that she held the little gorilla by her hands and swung her around until they were both dizzy.

Today Dotty can be seen spending a lot of time playing with Cassie while her "mom" Pongi rests. Sometimes she hangs on tightly to Jumoke while taking piggyback rides around the "gorilla villa." Other times she leans up against the gentle Mumbah while they enjoy a morning snack together, or she chuckles while Pongi tickles her belly. One thing is certain—Dotty has been welcomed with open arms into her new gorilla group.

GORILLA FACTS:
The Rest of the Story

WELL, I'LL BE A ~~MONKEY'S~~ GORILLA'S UNCLE!

Mumbah's gentle personality is unmistakable. He's so relaxed that you usually find him slumped against the bars of his cage, his lower lip hanging, his yellow teeth exposed. Born in the jungles of Cameroon in the 1960s, he was captured and taken to Howlett's Zoo Park in Canterbury, England, where he is believed to have sired two offspring.

The Columbus Zoo's favorite gorilla uncle, Mumbah

In August 1984 Mumbah was moved to the Columbus Zoo, but he has sired no offspring in Ohio. Instead, Mumbah has been like the cool uncle everyone likes to hang out with. His patient and tolerant demeanor have made him the perfect surrogate father for many young gorillas—Macombo, Mosuba, Jumoke, Nia, Nkosi, Kebi, Cassie, J. J., Fossey, Dotty, and Kambera.

Mumbah leads, keeps order, protects, teaches, and plays in his own unique way. The little gorillas gather around him, falling up against him and at times playing on him like he's a living jungle gym. Because of him,

95

these little ones have grown up feeling safe and secure—and Uncle Mumbah never complains about the little ones that just keep on coming.

BFF—Best Friends Forever

Before moving to the Columbus Zoo, a gorilla named Susie lived alone in a concrete cage at the Birmingham Zoo. A wild-born gorilla, she had been captured in Africa in the mid-1960s, and since her capture, Susie's most constant companion was a zookeeper named Randy Reid.

Twenty years later, an opportunity arose for Susie. The well-known zoo in Columbus, Ohio, had room for another female. She would finally get to live with a gorilla troop and have her own young.

"When you're working with an animal like this, you establish a relationship, and when it has to be severed, it's pretty much an emotional thing," Randy Reid said. "You lose part of your life. You lose one of your better friends. It's difficult to deal with. But I knew she was going to a better place. I knew it was something for her benefit. And whatever was for her benefit, I was for that."

Susie blended well with her new troop in Columbus. "Susie" had been her nickname, so she was given back her original name—Pongi. She and her silverback mate, Oscar, had two babies in four years. And Pongi adopted Dotty, adding to their troop. Although Randy knew that Susie's life had changed for the better, he still missed his old friend.

Three and a half years after their separation, Randy went to the Columbus Zoo to visit his old friend. She was in her outside enclosure when he arrived. He cupped his hands around his mouth and called out a name the gorilla hadn't heard in years: "Susie, c'mon, Sus. Come here. That a girl. How's my baby, Sus?"

When she heard the familiar voice, Pongi turned and ran to him. Through the wire fence, she reached out and cupped Randy behind his neck and hugged him to her. She put her face close to his and made soft purring sounds. Randy reached through the fence and rubbed the back of her head. It was an emotional reunion for both of them. Then she showed her new baby to him. Baby Colby looked up at Randy and took him by the hand.

Randy Reid said that people ask him, "Are the gorillas friendly to you?" He answers, "They are some of my best friends. I could trust Susie more than I could trust a person walking down the street."

Even after years of separation and having her name changed, Pongi recognized the voice of Randy Reid, her first keeper when he called her by her old nickname, Susie.

Babs and baby Bana at the Brookfield Zoo in Chicago

8

BABS: A GORILLA GOOD-BYE

The mood at the Brookfield Zoo in Chicago, Illinois, was somber on December 6, 2004. Babs, a thirty-year-old western lowland gorilla, had died after a long battle with kidney disease. Just as humans do, Babs left behind relatives and companions with whom she had a shared history. Led by a silverback named Ramar, Babs' troop included her mother, Alpha; Bana, a female whom Babs had given birth to nine years earlier; a sixteen-year-old female, Binti Jua; one of Binti's female offspring, nine-year-old Koola; Koola's baby, Kamba; and Nadaya, a three-year-old male from Babs's line.

Babs had been the matriarch, or dominant female, of her troop. When Baraka, Babs's oldest female offspring, died at the age of thirteen, Babs became the surrogate mother to Baraka's baby, Nadaya. Babs protected him when any of the other group members became too rough with him, and every night, she shared her nest with the young gorilla. Sometimes she carried Nadaya around the exhibit, even though he was old enough to move about on his own.

Being the older, more experienced mother, Babs had also "mentored" younger females on motherhood. When Koola had her baby, Kamba, Babs taught the new mother how to behave. Babs also spent a lot of time with Kamba, showering the newest addition to the troop with attention.

But as her illness worsened, Babs spent less time caring for Nadaya and the others, and more time resting. Bana often lay beside Babs on the mountain in their enclosure. Other times, Nadaya, rested at Babs's side, keeping her company.

After Babs's death, the Brookfield Zoo staff worried about her troop. The keepers had been caring for them every day, and they knew these gorillas were a close-knit bunch. They wondered if a visitation, or "gorilla wake," would benefit the surviving gorillas. In our culture, we say good-bye to our loved ones through wakes and funerals. It only seemed fair to give Babs's troop the same opportunity.

Once the decision to allow the gorillas to view the body was made, the keepers opened the doors of the Tropic World building to admit the members of Babs's gorilla troop. Nine-year-old Bana was the first to approach her mother's lifeless body.

"It was heartbreaking to see," said Amy Coons, a gorilla keeper for the past six years. "Bana came in with a stunned look on her face."

Babs's mother followed, along with the other female, Binti Jua. Nadaya came in with Koola and Koola's baby. Ramar, the silverback, stayed away.

Bana sat by Babs's head, holding one of her mother's hands in her own and stroking her mother's stomach with the other. "Then she laid down on the floor next to Babs, putting her head on Babs's outstretched arm," said veteran keeper Betty Green. "It was like they used to do in the exhibit, lying side by side on the mountain. Then Bana rose up and looked at us and moved to Babs's other side, tucked her head under the other arm, and stroked Babs's stomach."

The other gorillas also came to sniff Babs and gently touch the body. "Koola inspected Babs's mouth for a while and then held her baby close to Babs, like she used to do the last couple of months, letting Babs admire her," Green said.

"Nadaya was like a kid at a funeral. While [Babs] was ill, he had spent a lot of time resting with her. He came down and inspected and touched her, but moved away pretty quickly, playing with a sweet potato and just sitting and watching from a distance.

Babs and Bana shared a close bond.

"Alpha, Babs's mother, acted a little strangely. She did a couple of displays, by running in front of Babs's body, [grabbing] her legs, and then [running] past. She did that four times, not violently or moving the body, but like she was trying to wake Babs up."

Craig Demitros, the lead keeper who has been with the Brookfield Zoo's gorillas for the past twenty years, said, "We don't know if there is any benefit to the animals by doing this or not. We didn't think it would hurt. In the wild, gorillas are known to pay their respects in a similar fashion." The gorillas remained with Babs for about half an hour, and then they went back to the public display area to join their male leader, Ramar.

"Bana was the last to go," Coons said. "She would get up, move a few steps, stop, and turn back to stare at Babs. She started and stopped several times before she finally joined the others."

Each member of Babs's troop dealt with the loss in his or her own way, just as humans do.

CONCLUSION :
The True Heart of the Beast

Due to their strength, size, large jaws, and sharp teeth, gorillas have unfortunately long been misunderstood as ferocious, unfeeling beasts. Many believe the heart of the beast is merely an organ pumping blood through a creature that is incapable of feelings. Some believe that animals are only capable of feeling emotions, such as fear, that help them survive.

So how do we explain Colo's tenderness toward little J. J.? Or Willie B.'s joy at his newfound freedom, Bongo and Snowflake's loving devotion to their families, Pongi's compassion for the orphaned Dotty, and the sorrow and grief felt by Koko and Babs's troop after losing loved ones?

It is true that humans have the advantage of using words to convey their feelings, but members of the animal kingdom have unique ways of expressing themselves, too. After years of study and research, it is

Snowflake gives a hug.

A gorilla mother tenderly holds her infant.

now believed that gorillas think in abstract terms, express emotions, and communicate through posture, vocalizations, gestures, and actions. Anthropologist Beth Armstrong says, "Gorillas are a mirror of ourselves from the complexity of their social lives, to the rearing of their young, to their obvious sense of loss when losing a loved one."

To truly understand an animal, we should consider its emotional life with all of the feelings, such as grief, love, fear, anger, and sadness. We humans use the word "heart" when we talk about strength and tenderness. If a person shows compassion or dedication, he or she is said to have a lot of heart. If a person is hurting inside, we say that his or her heart is breaking. Although long misunderstood, a gorilla is truly a unique combination of strength and tenderness. And if we dare to listen, we, too, may hear the heart of the beast.

Young gorillas remain close to their mothers for several years after they are born.

A HISTORY OF THE BEAST:
Timeline

(Courtesy of the Wildlife Conservation Society's Bronx Zoo)

1846—While traveling in Gabon, European missionaries Savage and Wilson write the first description of a gorilla.

1861—Paul Belloni du Chaillu was the first person to "bag" or catch a gorilla. He described the gorilla as "half-man, half-beast."

1902—While climbing Mt. Sabingo in Uganda, a German officer, Captain von Beringe, shoots two mountain gorillas.

1912—Influenced by terrifying accounts of gorillas, researcher R. H. Garner conducts studies of gorillas from the safety of a cage while working in Gabon.

1921—Taxidermist Carl Akeley hunts five gorillas for the American Museum of Natural History during expeditions to the Virunga Mountains in Congo. The team weighs and measures the deceased animals. Afterwards, Akeley finds himself so affected by the wildlife of Africa that he and his wife move to Congo, and he becomes the first gorilla conservationist.

1925—Carl Akeley is instrumental in convincing the Belgian government to create a protected area for gorillas. Albert National Park is the first national park designated for the safe haven of gorillas in Africa.

A female mountain gorilla beats her chest

1959—George Schaller's landmark study of gorillas' behavior and ecology reveals gorillas as gentle creatures with strong family ties, finally debunking the myth of gorillas as vicious monsters. Schaller's methodology becomes a model for all future researchers studying gorillas. Methods include nest counting, tracking, and long-term observation.

1962—Albert National Park is divided as a result of the independence of Rwanda. It is split into two parks: the Volcano National Park in Rwanda and the Virunga National Park in Zaire.

Virunga National Park

1969—Forty percent of Volcano Park is converted into farmland. The European Union finances a project to grow pyrethrum, a peanut that produces a biodegradable insecticide. The value of this crop drops drastically just a few years later when the insecticide can be produced synthetically.

1973—The first complete census of Virunga mountain gorillas is completed by European researchers Harcourt and Groom. It reveals the population to be about 275 animals.

1977—Digit, a favorite gorilla of researcher Dian Fossey, is killed by poachers. Gorilla hands and skulls are sought by European tourists, resulting in a significant increase in poaching for gorilla parts. International attention to the threat to gorillas leads to an increase in the number of park guards.

1978—Amy Vedder and Bill Weber conduct mountain gorilla research.

1983—The Mountain Gorilla Project is in its third successful year, and local support for gorilla conservation is increased. Through education, the native people take pride in their gorillas. Guards are trained to protect the gorilla population from poachers.

1985—Researcher and gorilla advocate Dian Fossey is brutally murdered in her cabin at Karisoke. She is buried near her favorite gorillas. Her study site is operated by the Dian Fossey Gorilla Fund International, and it remains a center for gorilla research.

1989—Gorilla tourism becomes the third largest source of income for Rwanda. Local support increases. After ten successful years in Rwanda, the Mountain Gorilla Project expands to Uganda and Zaire. It is now known as the International Gorilla Conservation Project.

1994—Civil war breaks out in Rwanda. In Zaire, hundreds of thousands of refugees make camps at the base of the mountain gorilla habitat. For daily survival, the refugees hunt gorillas and take wood from the national park.

Refugees flee to escape fighting in their homeland.

A troop of wild mountain gorillas

1997—Experts note the first rise in the mountain gorilla population since the conservation program began in 1980.

2004—Good news! According to a 2004 census of mountain gorillas in the Virunga Volcanoes, the critically endangered population is growing. In 1989, the estimated population was 324 individuals. In 2004, that number rose by fifty-six individuals, or seventeen percent, to 380 individual gorillas. The Virunga gorilla census was conducted by six teams traveling across the entire habitat range, searching for signs—including nests and actual mountain gorilla sightings—to establish the number of gorillas in each troop.

The future—Historically, gorillas have been threatened by poaching, loss of habitat, civil unrest, and disease. But conservation efforts are helping the gorillas make a comeback.

Let's GO on a GOrilla Safari

You'll need sunscreen, bug spray, a camera . . . and don't forget your wallet! To go on a gorilla safari, visitors pay guides to take them into parks and reserves, and they often buy food, beverages, and souvenirs as well. These profits from ecotourism—tourism that is focused on conservation—provide much-needed income for poor, rural areas that are rich in natural resources. But more importantly, if local communities see direct economic benefits from gorilla tourism, they are more likely to protect these endangered animals and conserve their precious habitat—and won't need to force gorillas off the land in order to use it in other ways, such as farming, logging, or development.

Guides take groups of tourists to view gorillas in their natural habitat.

FOR FURTHER READING

Ake, Anne. *The Gorilla*. Lucent Overview Series: Endangered Animals & Habitats. San Diego: Lucent Books, Inc., 1999.

Arndt, Laura M. Sanders. *Can Rwandans, mountain gorillas and tourists coexist?* Aurora, CO: Eaglecrest High School, 1992.

Carroll, Richard. "In the Garden of the Gorilla." *Wildlife Conservation*, May/June, 1990.

Cavalieri, Paola and Peter Singer. *The Great Ape Project: Equality Beyond Humanity*. New York: St. Martin's Press, 1993.

Dennard, Deborah. *Gorillas*. Chanhassen, MN: NorthWord Press, 2002.

Fine, Douglas. 1995. The misty future of Rwanda's mountain gorillas. *Washington Post*, 30 April.

Fleisher, Paul. *Gorillas*. Tarrytown, NY: Benchmark Books, 2001.

Johnstone, Marianne. *Gorillas and Their Babies*. A Zoo Life Book. New York: Rosen/ Power Kids Press, 1999.

Lindsay, Jennifer. *The Great Apes*. New York: MetroBooks, 1999.

McCollum, Sean. "Ape Adoption." *National Geographic Kids*, October 2005, 7.

McRae, Michael. "Orphan Gorillas: Will They Survive in the Wild?" *National Geographic*, February 2000, 84-97.

Matthews, Tom L. *Light Shining through the Mist: A Photobiography of Dian Fossey*. Washington, D.C.: National Geographic Society, 1998.

Milton, Joyce. *Gorillas: Gentle Giants of the Forest*. New York: Random House, 1997.

Ritchie, Rita. *Mountain Gorillas in Danger*. 1991. Reprint, Boston: Houghton Mifflin, 1999.

Redmond, Ian. *Gorillas*. Wildlife at Risk. New York: Bookwright Press, 1991.

—. *Gorilla, Monkey & Ape*. New York: Dorling Kindersley, 2000.

Rock, Maxine. *Kishina: A True Story of Gorilla Survival*. Atlanta: Peachtree Publishers, 1996.

Schaller, George B. *The Mountain Gorilla: Ecology and Behavior*. 1963. Reprint, Chicago: University of Chicago Press, 1976.

Schott, Jane A. *Dian Fossey and the Mountain Gorillas*. Minneapolis: Carolrhoda Books, 1999.

Simon, Seymour. *Gorillas*. New York: HarperCollins, 2000.

Sleeper, Barbara. *Primates: The Amazing World of Lemurs, Monkeys, and Apes*. San Francisco: Chronicle Books, 1997.

Sunderland-Groves, Jacqueline. "Cross River Gorillas." *Wildlife Conservation* 109, no 2. (March/April 2006): 8-9.

Wexo, John Bonnett. *Gorillas*. Mankato, MN: Creative Education Publishers, 1991.

"Wild Gorillas Take Time for Tool Use." *Science News* 168, no. 16 (October 15, 2005): 253.

SPECIAL ACKNOWLEDGEMENTS

The Columbus Zoo: Thanks to Don Winstell and Jack Hanna for opening the doors to the Columbus Zoo and to all of the wonderful keepers, especially Dan Nellis and Barbara Jones, who always took the time to help and share their passion for gorillas. I'd like to thank my good friend Charlene Jendry for sharing her knowledge and love of gorillas and for reading my manuscripts. Thanks to Sheila Campbell, the librarian at the Columbus Zoo, for her help. I would also like to thank Debbie Elder, Mary Anne Huber, Adelle Dodge, Norma Dodge, Mandy Demczyk, Dusty Lombardi, Erin Schuler, Jennifer Compston, Rick Prebeg, and Dr. Michael Barrie. And many thanks to Michael Pogany for believing in this book and helping with the wonderful photographs.

Also, thanks to Charles Horton from **Zoo Atlanta**, Maria Teresa Abello from the **Barcelona Zoo,** and Richard Johnstone-Scott from the Jersey Zoo for sharing your wonderful stories of the gorillas you loved. Thanks to Allison Reiser and Vanessa Jones from the **Bronx Zoo,** Jane Dewar of **Gorilla Haven,** and Kristen Arnold from **Busch Gardens Zoo.** And a big thank-you to Tara Stoinski (**Zoo Atlanta**) and Erica Archibald (**Dian Fossey Gorilla Foundation**) for their knowledge and expertise. I want to thank Beth Armstrong from the **Brevard Zoo** for suggesting that there were many great gorilla stories out there, if I cared to look. Also, thanks to Mary Lane of WBNS-TV and Lindsay Woodland from *The Columbus Dispatch*.

My heartfelt thanks go to my editor and friend, Tanya Dean, whose perseverance and unwavering support in this project was amazing. And many thanks to Kristen Kapustar, Maggie Smith, Kelly Rabideau, and John Margeson for all of their hard work and dedication. Moreover, thanks to Kelly Milner Halls, who has an uncanny way of lighting a fire under me to get me to believe in myself over and over again—and to Stephanie Greene whose constant support keeps me smiling and writing. You are special people in my life.

Hugs and thanks to my mom, who believed in this book before anyone else. Thanks to all of my good friends who have put up with me "going ape" over gorillas. And last, but not least, thanks for the love and support of my family, my husband, Ed, and my three beautiful daughters, Allison, Lindsay, and Carli.

—Nancy Roe Pimm

BIBLIOGRAPHY

INTERVIEWS

Armstrong, Beth. Anthropologist, Brevard Zoo, Melbourne, Florida. Interviewed August 10, 2005, and March 9, 2006.

Dodge, Martha. Zoo Docent, Columbus Zoo. Interviewed March 2, 2006.

Elder, Debbie. Gorilla Zookeeper, Columbus Zoo. Interviewed March 3, 2006.

Horton, Charles. Curator for Great Apes, ZooAtlanta. Interviewed January 11, 2006.

Huber, Mary Anne. Zoo Docent and Historian, Columbus Zoo. Interviewed September 27, 2005.

Jendry, Charlene. Conservationist, Columbus Zoo and Partners in Conservation. Interviewed August 16, 2005.

Jones, Barbara. Gorilla Zookeeper, Columbus Zoo. Interviewed March 14, 2006.

Jones, Barbara and Maureen Casale. Gorilla Zookeepers, Columbus Zoo. Interviewed October 17, 2004.

Nellis, Dan. Gorilla Zookeeper, Columbus Zoo. Interviewed February 8, 2005.

ARTICLES

Armstrong, Beth. "Bongo: A Keeper's Reflections." *Gorilla Gazette* 4, no. 3 (December 1990): 8-9.

Abello, Maria Teresa. "Snowflake: A Unique Gorilla and Grandfather." *Gorilla Gazette* 17, no. 1 (April 2004): 1.

Fossey, Dian. "Making Friends with Mountain Gorillas." *National Geographic*, January 1970, 48-67.

Fuchs, Dale. 2003. Rare gorilla dead. *New York Times*, November 25.

Irvine, Garth. "Zoo Gorilla Diets." *Gorilla Gazette* 17, no. 1 (April 2004): 59.

Knowlton, H. H. 1988. Male gorilla fine example of what a parent should be. *Columbus Dispatch*. June 26.

Knudson, Tara. "One of a Kind." *Boy's Quest*, February 2003, 32.

Mullen, William. 2004. One by one, gorillas pay their last respects. *Chicago Tribune*, December 8.

——. 2005. Gorillas take stab at mind games. *Chicago Tribune*, October 30.

Paprocki, Ray. "Bongo," *Columbus Monthly*, December 1990, 74-80.

Richards, Corlyss. "They Will Show Us; Have We the Vision?" *Columbus Zoo & Aquarium Docent Newsletter*. October 1996, 12.

Switzer, John. 1987. Mother gorilla dies; Father, baby mourn. *Columbus Dispatch*, October 8.

——. 1988. The big gorilla is quite a dad—Bongo's motherless son gets his closest attention. *Columbus Dispatch*, June 16.

Warner, Jack. 1989. Willie B.'s first date. *Atlanta Journal Constitution*, May 3.

——. 1994. Willie B.'s first baby. *Atlanta Journal Constitution*, February 10.

Wild, Abigail. 2003. Gorilla in the midst. *Herald* (Glasgow), September 26.

WEB SOURCES

Ambassador Willie B. http://www.zooatlanta.org/animals_willieb.htm

Daughter of Sunshine http://www.angelfire.com/pa/busterboo/sunshine.html

Dewar, Jane. "Famous Gorillas." Gorilla Haven. http://www.gorillahaven.org/ghfamous.htm

Dewar Wildlife Trust. "Silverback Award." Gorilla Haven. http://www.gorilla-haven.org/ghsilverbackaward.htm

——. "Some Fun Info and Facts About Gorillas for Kids Big and Small." Gorilla Haven. http://www.gorillahaven.org/ghfunfacts.htm

The Family Tree of Willie B. http://www.zooatlanta.org/animals_willieb_family_album.htm

Koko's Kids Club http://www.koko.org/kidsclub/learn/10facts.html

Larsen, Janet. "Our Closest Relatives are Disappearing." Earth Policy Institute, March 5, 2002. http://www.earthpolicy.org/Updates/Update7.htm

Mountain Gorilla: Information from Answers.com http://www.answers.com/topic/mountain-gorilla-1

Nitsch, Marianne. "Bachelor Gorilla Groups in European Zoos." AG Human Biology and Anthropology. Institute of Biology. Division of Biology, Chemistry, Pharmacy. Freie Universität, Berlin, Germany. http://www.biologie.fu-berlin.de/humanbio/publnit.htm

Durrell, Gerald. "The Hero Jambo." The Ark Gallery. http://shoarns.com/Jambo.html

BOOKS

Braithwaite, Althea. *Gorillas*. Save Our Wildlife. Chicago: Longman Group, 1988.

De La Bédoyère, Camilla. *No One Loved Gorillas More*. Washington, D.C.: National Geographic Society, 2005.

Demuth, Patricia. *Gorillas*. New York: Grosset & Dunlap, 1994.

Dennard, Deborah. *Gorillas*. Chanhassen, Minnesota: NorthWord Press, 2002.

Dunbar, Robin and Louise Barrett. *Cousins: Our Primate Relatives*. London: Dorling Kindersley, 2000.

Fleisher, Paul. *Gorillas*. Tarrytown, New York: Benchmark Books, 2001.

Fossey, Dian. *Gorillas in the Mist*. Boston: Houghton Mifflin Company, 1983.

Freedman, Suzanne. *Dian Fossey— Befriending the Gorillas*. Austin, TX: Raintree Steck-Vaughn Publishers, 1997.

Hanna, Jack. *Monkeys on the Interstate: And Other Tales from America's Favorite Zookeeper*. New York: Doubleday, 1989.

Harrison, Virginia. *Mountain Gorillas and Their Young*. Milwaukee: Gareth Stevens Children's Books, 1991.

Irvine, Georgeanne. *Raising Gordy Gorilla at the San Diego Zoo*. New York: Simon & Schuster Books for Young Readers, 1990.

Johnstone-Scott, Richard. *Jambo, A Gorilla's Story*. London: Michael O'Mara Books Ltd., 1995.

Kalman, Bobbie & Heather Levigne. *What is a Primate?* New York: Crabtree Publishing Co., 1999.

Levy-Bruhl, L. *Les functions mentales dans les sociéties inferiéurs*. Paris: Felix Alcan, 1910.

Lewin, Ted & Betsy. *Gorilla Walk*. New York: Lothrop, Lee, & Shepard Books, 1999.

Lyttle, Jeff. *Gorillas in Our Midst: The Story of the Columbus Zoo Gorillas*. Columbus, OH: Ohio State University Press, 1997.

Martin, Patricia Fink. *Gorillas*. New York: Children's Press, 2000.

McNulty, Faith. *With Love from Koko*. New York: Scholastic Inc., 1990.

Miller-Schroeder, Patricia. *Gorillas*. Austin, TX: Raintree Steck-Vaughn Publishers, 1997.

Milner Halls, Kelly. *Albino Animals*. Plain City, OH: Darby Creek Publishing, 2004.

Milton, Joyce. *Gorillas, Gentle Giants of the Forest*. New York: Random House, 1997.

Montgomery, Sy. *Walking with the Great Apes*. Boston: Houghton Mifflin, 1991.

Moussaieff Masson, Jeffrey and Susan McCarthy. *When Elephants Weep: The Emotional Lives of Animals*. New York: Delacorte Press, 1995.

Patterson, Dr. Francine. *Koko's Story*. New York: Scholastic, Inc., 1987.

——. *Koko-Love! Conversations with a Signing Gorilla*. New York: Dutton Children's Books, 1999.

——. *Koko's Kitten*. New York: Scholastic, 1985.

Patterson, Dr. Francine and Eugene Linden. *The Education of Koko*. New York: Holt, Rinehart, & Winston, 1981.

Redmond, Ian. *Gorilla*. New York: Knopf, 1995.

——. *Gorilla, Monkey, & Ape*. New York: Dorling Kindersly, 1995.

Regan, Tom and Peter Singer (eds.). *Animal Rights and Human Obligations*. Englewood Cliffs, New Jersey: Prentice-Hall, 1989.

Roberts, Jack. *Dian Fossey*. San Diego: Lucent Books, 1995.

Schlein, Miriam. *Jane Goodall's Animal World: Gorillas*. New York: Atheneum, 1990.

Simon, Seymour. *Gorillas*. New York: HarperCollins Publishers, 2000.

Taylor, Marianne. *Animals Under Threat: Mountain Gorilla*. Chicago: Heinemann Library, 2004.

Wexo, John Bonnett. *Gorillas*. Mankato, Minnesota: Creative Education Publishers, 1991.

VIDEOS

The Gorilla Foundation. *Koko's Kitten*. VHS. Los Angeles: Churchill Films, 1989.

National Geographic Explorer. *Urban Gorilla*. National Geographic Video, 1991.

National Geographic Society and WQED Pittsburgh. *Gorilla*. National Geographic Video, 1982.

Staley, Nancy. *The Columbus Zoo Gorillas: A Primate Family*. Columbus Zoo and Aquarium: 1985.

Tigress Productions Limited and Thirteen/WNET New York. *Nature: Snowflake: The White Gorilla*. DVD. PBS, 2005.

WSB-TV Atlanta. *The Life and Times of Willie B*. Cox Enterprises, 2001.

INDEX